How to Make Money as a Freelance Writer

John Lynch

© John Lynch 2016

John Lynch has asserted his moral right under the Copyright, Designs and Patents Act 1988 to be identified as the author of this work.

Published by Mandrill Press www.mandrillpress.com

ISBN 978-1-910194-19-5

Edited and proofread by Kirstie Edwards www.kirstieedwards.eu

Author photograph by Ruth Jenkinson Photography

Cover design by the author

ALSO BY JOHN LYNCH
Historical Fiction
A Just and Upright Man by R J Lynch
Poor Law by R J Lynch

Contemporary Fiction
Zappa's Mam's a Slapper by John Lynch
Sharon Wright: Butterfly by John Lynch

Non-Fiction
Managing the High Tech Salesforce by John Lynch
The International Sales Handbook by John Lynch

Preface

When I retired in May 2015 after a long career in international sales, I knew that doing nothing was not an option. In my forties, I'd dreamed – as so many do – of retirement as years of idleness with a little gardening, some cycling, travel to warm places in cold months and a lot of reading. By the time I reached retirement age, I knew myself better than that.

I'd lived and worked on every continent except Antarctica. I'd be in my hotel room late in the evening, writing notes on the calls I'd made that day and preparing my presentations for the next. At four the next morning I'd be up again and writing once more – this time "my stuff": short stories and full-length novels, because as well as a long-time salesman I'd been a writer since I was ten years old. I couldn't simply stop. It would kill me. Perhaps literally.

So what to do? I had my savings and my pension, so I could do those things I'd dreamed of doing – but, as it turned out, I didn't want to do them. I did go on writing fiction because I couldn't stop – but fiction writing is a lonely occupation and I'm a gregarious person. Writing novels was not going to be enough. I decided to revisit something I had been doing on and off since selling an article to Good Housekeeping Magazine in 1989. I'd revive my career as a freelance writer, but this time I'd do it seriously. If I wasn't successful, and successful by standards I'd set for myself, I'd stop freelancing. The figure I set was £2,000 (US$3,300) a month before tax. If I couldn't earn that from freelancing, I'd count myself a failure, give up and find something else to do.

That may sound an unambitious target – it's less than the national average wage – but I haven't had a mortgage for years and school fees are also a thing of the past, so it was enough to pay every normal household bill. Add to that my other target, which was to freelance for only three hours a day (though I mean every day – seven days a week) because I wanted to leave plenty of time for what I thought of as "my stuff", by which I mean writing novels and short stories, and £2,000 looks a lot more sensible.

There was no shortage of advice and all of it told me I was wasting my time. The bottom had fallen out of the freelance writing business. Fees had been driven close to zero by a huge influx of writers proficient in English who lived in countries where the cost of living was minuscule, and by clients who would always accept the lowest bid. There wasn't the work around that once there had been. Even an eternal optimist like me must be able to see that the project was a waste of time.

Well, it's true – I am an optimist. And right to be, because I hit my income target for the first time in month two and I haven't missed it since. If I'd been prepared to work six hours a day instead of three, I'd have doubled the money. The doom mongers who said there wasn't enough work were wrong – there was masses of it that hadn't been there even ten years earlier. And, yes, there are a huge number of people who call themselves freelance writers. A lot don't reach the standard that clients need, and neither do they do the work necessary to succeed.

I've written this book to do two things. The first is to explain what that standard is, and the second is to tell you what you have to do if you want to make a living wage as a freelance writer (and, believe me, it's a lot easier to do that as a freelance writer than as a novelist). I'm happy to share this information because – whatever you may hear – for the happy few, there's actually more decently paying work around than we can handle.

Want to join us? Read on.

Chapter 1

Introduction

I'm writing this on the opening day of 2016. I wrote my first piece as a freelance writer 27 years ago in 1989. That was an article for *Good Housekeeping* magazine (I didn't realise then that I was starting at the top with a long way to fall if things went wrong). In 1990 I wrote a book called *Managing the High Tech Salesforce* and began a stint as Writer For Hire (a slightly posher expression for freelance writer) that lasted four years during which I wrote two full-length books, a number of video scripts, eight training courses and too many flyers and promotional pieces to count – all for the same company.

I took a break then because I was offered a three month interim management project in my previous work as an international sales director that turned, in the way these things do, into 15 years of full-time employment, though I went on writing and during that time published three novels and a non-fiction book (The International Sales Handbook). This book you have in your hand is a How-To book and the lesson you should take from this paragraph is: freelancers are flexible. They turn their hand to whatever comes up.

When I retired from international sales in May last year, I wasn't ready to stop work entirely. I'm still writing fiction, but I wanted to do more – so I decided to resurrect my freelance writing career. I set myself two targets: to work as a freelancer for no more than three hours a day to leave time for my fiction and for the other things I like to do; and to cover all of my expenses from after-tax freelance income alone, keeping my pension and savings for more important things. My days of paying mortgages and school fees ended some time ago but there's still the little matter of housekeeping, insurance and utilities and the upshot of my deliberations was that I needed to earn not less than £2,000 (US$3,300) a month before tax.

If I had listened to what experienced people told me, I would have accepted that in the current market there was no way I was ever going to achieve my aim. Lots of people will tell you that freelance writers can no longer make a living. And they are wrong. It can be done. I hit my target in Month 2 and I haven't stopped hitting it since then. And I'm turning business away because I don't want to burn out and I do want to be sure I have enough time to write what I think of as "my stuff", which means my fiction.

I'd like to propose a division of freelance work into three parts:
- Working for "content mills"

- Pay-per-word work that has a more respectable pay rate than "content mills"
- Traditional freelance work involving research and paid at National Union of Journalists (NUJ) or other recognised rates.

For the sake of people who haven't heard the expression "content mills," I'll explain this.

Content Mill

The phenomenal growth of the Web and its appetite for words has combined with the availability of "writers", more often than not from the Indian subcontinent, whose grasp of English idiom, grammar, sentence construction and the like fails to match the standard they think it reaches. What they write is, to be blunt, not very good though, to be fair, they don't know that and it doesn't matter anyway because there are lots of customers happy to take content that isn't very good onto their websites and blogs in the mistaken belief that only SEO matters and that the rubbish they offer the world boosts their search engine rankings. There's nothing to be done about that; customers will continue to offer jobs at one penny a word and "writers" will continue to accept them. I talk about Copify and Upwork and the other content mills in Chapter 4; despite what some freelancers will tell you it isn't a disgrace to work for them (though it is likely to bore you to tears and to feel like a terrible chore) so if you want to, this book will tell you how.

Higher Paid Web Content

If you like, you can think of this as "premium content mill" work. It's available on Upwork and from other sources (see Chapter 4) and I do quite a lot of it. There's very little research involved – you get the job, you write the piece, you send it in and you get paid. Rates are anywhere from three cents to eight cents a word. To put that in context, five cents a word at the rate at which I write *provided there is no time out to research* amounts to $60 an hour and that's a respectable rate for most people and certainly more than NUJ rates.

"Traditional" Freelancing

I use that expression to describe writing for magazines and newspapers. I do as much of that as I can; if I could, I would do nothing else but the ratio of good journalists to available work is such that almost no writer can get as much as they need. Once again, Chapter 4 is where I talk about how to find this work.

Google "freelance writer" or "freelance writing" and you'll turn up an awful lot of stuff. It will include articles decrying the content mills and saying that the writer never takes on a job at less than, say, a dollar a word. And, for traditional freelancing, that makes sense – I expect an absolute minimum of 50p a word for that work because I have to cover the cost of time spent in research, and if the research is going to be extensive then I want more than that. However, you do need to take some of what you read with a pinch of salt. Not long ago, I received an email (and it will have gone to everyone whose address she has) from someone whose website links to an article extolling the virtues of "not working for peanuts" and insisting on a minimum of a dollar a word. However, although this person appeared to champion turning work away at less than a dollar a word, her email asked for help; she had to replace a failed PC and simply couldn't afford to do it, so she asked how her readership would feel about making a donation. Well. Hmm. Okay. Personally, I'm writing this on a rather nice Lenovo T450s running Windows 10 and Microsoft Office 2016 which I paid for out of the surplus from one month's freelancing (not even earning a dollar a word). Sometimes, you have to say, "I'll stick to what I know works."

I split my time between writing for newspapers and magazines at NUJ rates and taking the better paid Web jobs. For the latter, what I settled on after a while was that I'd aim to write as a freelance a minimum of 2,000 words a day and a maximum of 3,000 words a day at an average rate of 4p or four cents a word (in general, good British clients pay a little better than good American clients, possibly because the cost of living and the average income are both higher in the UK) and I'd do it seven days a week. It's working out just fine; bit by bit, I dropped the clients who weren't paying enough and refused to take on any who wouldn't meet my price. I didn't drop anyone, though, without giving them four weeks' notice so that they could make other arrangements. They were all decent people and I thought that was only fair. And I recently put the minimum rate I'd accept up to 5p a word but I felt able to do that because my diary is pretty full. Begin by getting the amount of work you want and building up the portfolio you need. Then put your prices up.

I'll have more to say later in the book about turning business away – mostly about choosing which requests you're not going to accept and making sure that, however busy you are, you never stop putting yourself out there (because what happens if one of your main clients walks under a bus? Or just doesn't like you anymore?)

Please note: I said it can be done. I did not say that anyone could do it. A huge number of people who call themselves freelance writers don't earn enough to buy a decent meal for two at the end of the week. The purpose of this book is to tell you how to become one of the happy few. But first you need to know whether you have it in you. Turn to Chapter 2 and let's get started.

Chapter 2

People say there's no work worth having for freelance writers. Are they wrong?

People do say there's no work worth having for freelance writers and I understand why they say it but they are wrong. There are two reasons for the belief that freelance writing is an unrewarding waste of time. The first has to do with the large number of journalists who have been made redundant by newspapers and magazines around the world and now seek to make a living doing what they were doing before, but doing it as freelancers. The second (and I'd better make it clear that I'm talking about English language freelancing and no other kind) has to do with the number of people who claim fluency as writers of English and live in countries where the cost of living is so low that they can bid very low prices for a job.

I'll deal with these in order.

Journalism

First, the journalist thing. I know that many people with ambitions as freelance writers think they'll only have reached their goal when they have an NUJ card and they are writing commissioned pieces for magazines with big circulations and national newspapers. Well, I do some of that and I do it at NUJ rates, but most of what I do is anonymous, appears on other people's websites and blogs and is paid by the word. And that will be true for you, too, unless you have impeccable credentials in a big-selling niche market. So most of this book is going to be about selling material that will appear on the Web and won't have your name on it.

Journalists will tell you that there are too many people chasing not enough work and trying to win it from editors who want to pay too little money (and, increasingly, don't want to get round to paying at all). All of that is true. If you want to place a story with a regular news outlet and you don't have a background as a journalist and contacts you made while working as one, you will have to work very hard to succeed and you may decide it's not worth the trouble of trying. (Though it *is* worth the trouble. Don't give up.) But writing news and opinion pieces for newspapers and magazines is journalism. Extrapolating from there being insufficient work for freelance journalists to saying that there is therefore no work for freelance writers ignores the explosion of the Web and its rapacious demand for what Web practitioners call "content".

And, in any case, it isn't true that there is no work for journalists. I submit ideas to the printed media, get some of them accepted, write the pieces and get paid. And I do it sufficiently often to feel able to say "I'm a journalist." I submitted one just this morning, as it happens, to a Lad's Mag with the title *From Harvest Festivals to the Thong*. It's a study (tongue in cheek) of how central heating has changed the design of ladies' underwear over the past 60 years. We'll see how it goes – but that's not what I rely on to pay the bills. I also have blog posts to write on:

- visiting Valle de Guadalupe during the fall
- digitising compliance in the Southern California transportation and warehousing industry
- public tragedy: make your social media response appropriate
- choosing the right window shade for your design scheme
- what to take with you on an upscale cycling holiday

Is that exciting or is that exciting? Well, no, I suppose it isn't. But there's variety there, the flow of work is steady and the pay will be more than adequate. If you're starting out, this is the sort of thing you need to be aiming for. The bylines and the movies about your life in investigative journalism can come later.

I'll be saying more in Chapter 4 about how to get business and I'll talk there about submitting ideas; for now, I'll focus on the mistake I made when I started and how I fixed it.

The mistake was not analysing at the outset what I had to sell that people might want to buy. I've worked all over the world but with a special emphasis on the Middle East and Africa. I know a lot about those places and I have opinions. Good for me; but newspaper editors didn't want to hear my opinions and they didn't want to publish them. I did get one piece published in a regional newspaper but it became clear that I was not going to do it often enough to keep pegging away. So I did some thinking.

What I thought about was: what do I know that there might be a market for and that not everyone knows? I'm suggesting that you do the same. In my case, I decided that my saleable knowledge was likely to be in these areas:

- overseas trade; the financing of it and the corruption it involves
- how to stay safe in dangerous places and still bring home the order
- the ways doing business varies between different countries (even countries very close to each other like Nigeria, Ghana and Sierra Leone)
- good ways to travel and places to stay (and, by extension, bad ways to travel and bad places to stay).

That was a start and I sold some articles. (More about how I did that, and how you can do it, in Chapter 4). It wasn't really enough, though, and now that I had the bit

between my teeth I started adding stuff. I joined IBM in 1967 and I was in the IT business for 25 years so I added:
- the development of IT from punched cards through large mainframes to PCs and on to the Cloud
- the major players, and how to spot a new trend before everyone is on board
- product life cycles that get shorter every year and the need for rapid payback.

As I've already said, after I left IT I spent four years as a writer for hire and then went back into sales. This time I was working in a more low-tech environment and I learned about:
- road safety; how to promote it; where it's good, where it leaves room for improvement and where it's diabolical. (By "where" in that sentence, I mean "in which countries". Don't ask me to travel on another road in Ethiopia, because I won't do it)
- bridges, with particular emphasis on bearings and bridge joints
- the paint, thermoplastic and other products used in marking roads and airports
- the relationship between manufacturers, contractors, consultants and governments

But hang on – what was I doing when I learned about these things? I was in sales; as salesman, sales manager and sales director. My very first published book was *Managing the High Tech Salesforce*. So I also knew about:
- sales techniques
- recruiting, managing, motivating, disciplining and (occasionally) firing salespeople
- analysing sales territories and negotiating sales targets

I probably sell three or four articles a month on one or more of the topics I've just listed. It wouldn't be enough on its own, but it goes very nicely with the other things I do and as time passes and I sell more I'm getting a reputation as the "go-to" writer in a couple of my specialist areas. I've sold articles that editors asked me for rather than only things that I myself proposed.

The list of areas I specialise in has grown too, because as I got better known I was asked to write on things I knew very little about and I made it my business to learn more. As a freelancer you have to become like a magpie, picking things up and storing them away and learning more about them.

Your list of specialist topics is going to be different from mine but don't tell me you don't have one, because you do. So let's find them. Here's an exercise which, if you're reading this in the paperback format, you can do right here on the pages I've provided. If you've got the e-book version, pick up a pad or a notebook and use that.

Of course I know that many readers will not want to write on these pages. They will find the very idea childish. I probably wouldn't fill them out myself if they were presented to me in this way because I hate the idea that I'm being talked down to as much as anyone does. And that's fine. What matters is that, like me, you find the things you know enough about to be able to sell them. Where you record the answers, even if it's only in your memory (as long as your memory doesn't resemble a sieve) doesn't really matter.

Take lots of time working through these questions. You want the most complete summary as possible of the things you have to sell. Like me, you'll probably come back to it a number of times when other things you hadn't previously thought of pop into your mind. That's fine. What you're doing here is building up the record of the things you're going to sell.

EXERCISE

BUILD A LIST OF THE SUBJECTS YOU CAN WRITE ABOUT

Q1. What subjects did you study at college, university or otherwise?

_____

_____

_____

_____

_____

_____

Q2. What employment, paid and unpaid, have you had?

_____

_____

_____

_____

_____

_____

Q3. What other life experiences have you had from which you learnt things?

_____

_____

_____

_____

_____

_____

Q4. Taking everything you've said about yourself and your history, what do you know that there might be a market for and that not everyone knows?

Okay, so now you have your list of subject areas on which you can claim to be knowledgeable. If you're not British, you probably won't find it difficult to tell the world about them; if you are, you may be reluctant to blow your trumpet. Get over it. You'll only start selling when the world knows what you have to offer and the world will only find out when you tell it.

And don't be shy. If you offer a piece to an editor, what's the worst that can happen? The editor can refuse it. Right? Editors are refusing pieces every day, and many of them from much bigger names than yours or mine, so being turned down is no big deal. When it happens, offer it to a different editor at another publication.

Sometimes, though, you'll have to just assume that it's been turned down because editors are even ruder than agents and publishers. If they want the piece, they'll contact you. If they don't, they won't. If you haven't heard within thirty-six hours, offer it somewhere else. And then ask yourself why you waited that long. It's fine, when you've submitted a piece to an editor, to contact them after three hours and ask if they're going to use it. But do that by email and not by phone because editors are unbelievably busy people.

The Web

There can't be a company or a business outside North Korea that doesn't have at least a website and probably also a blog (which may or may not be part of the website). Their primary interest is in SEO (Search Engine Optimisation), because without good SEO they won't appear on the first page when someone uses a search engine to look for a business like theirs and, if they don't get onto that first page, they are as good as invisible. Their business will suffer and perhaps die. In the complex set of factors that search engines look at to decide how to rank websites, the frequency with which a site is updated and the quality of those updates are both important. Somebody has to provide them.

Then there are reviews: product reviews; service reviews; anything can be reviewed and probably will be.

My guess is that the amount of published material (taking "published" in the broadest sense) is now three or four times and perhaps more what it was forty years ago, when some of those now redundant journalists had just started taking their Pitman shorthand courses.

Yes, much of what appears on websites is badly written, semi-literate, ungrammatical rubbish. But savvy operators are realising that this kind of substandard offering attracts no-one and there's a very real demand for writers who can offer a quality product.

Here's what I wrote in my *Guide to Finding a Freelance Writer*:

> Freelance writing in recent years has much in common with many other services: it's been outsourced to cheaper offshore providers. That has brought the cost down, but it's brought the quality down, too. Suppose you want a 500 word description of product quality, warranty or some similar matter. You can get those five hundred words written for £0.50. (Oh, yes, you can – I promise you). It will be done by someone with little experience to whom five hundred rupees (because that's what it will mean to them) will buy a meal on the streets of Mumbai and they'll be glad to have it. Why would you want to spend another £49.50 to get the job done by a native English speaker with a couple of decades' experience of writing this sort of thing? I think I've given you the answer to that.

And that answer is that the 50 pence offering won't be good enough to attract customers. Which is a very good lead-in to the next heading:

What do you need to be a freelance writer?

Forgive me for stating the obvious but to be a freelance writer you need, first of all, **to be able to write**.

I can hear the responses. "Well, I can read, can't I? I'm reading this book. If I can read, I can write. Duh!"

It isn't that simple. Here's an extract from my historical romance/crime book, A Just and Upright Man. It's set in the north-east of England in the 1760s and in this passage, labourer's daughter Kate Greener is talking to Mistress Wortley, the well-to-do widow of a lawyer, about Kate's desire to learn to read. (This will mean most to those who, like me, were brought up in the north-east and are used to the idea that people say "us" when they mean "me" and the rest of the sometimes odd way we have of speaking):

> 'Lady Isabella goes every summer to Harrogate. We pray in church for her safe return.'
> 'Yes, I can see that a provincial soul might warm to Harrogate. For me, Bath is not entirely without its compensations. And now, tell me. Why do you want to learn to read and write?'
> 'Miss, I want to better myself. I want to read the bible for myself, instead of hearing only what someone else thinks is important. And I'd like to know what's going on in the world.'
> 'Very well. Estimable wishes, so long as you do not think to rise above your station. But reading and writing are not enough. You must also learn to speak.'
> 'Speak, Miss? But, Miss, I speak every day. I am speaking to you now.'
> 'That is not speaking. You have much to learn. For now, let us content ourselves with but a few simple rules. You must not say us when you mean me. You must not say our Mam, but my mother. Or, better still, simply Mother. You will not call people Man, whatever sex they may be. And never, ever, shall you address someone as pet. Is that clear? There will be more to learn, when you have mastered this. I shall call you Katherine. You will call me Mistress Wortley, or Ma'am. And now, let us begin.'

Kate is affronted when Mistress Wortley says that what Kate thinks of as "speaking" is not what Mistress Wortley means by the term and I know that people are sometimes equally affronted when I suggest that what they mean by "writing" is not adequate to the purpose of earning a living as a freelance writer. Nevertheless, I stand by the view. Writing can take many different forms, and in this book we will encounter a number of them because different freelance tasks require different ways to write. I can think of at least six ways, all different, in which I write and the one I choose depends on what kind of writing I'm doing at the time.

Before this book is over, I'm going to have upset a number of people from the Indian subcontinent, who will be very happy to tell me and anyone else that their English is superb. And it often is. But it's superb as Indian English or Pakistani English or Bangladeshi English and, to be frank, there isn't a very high demand for that.

I saw a proposal a little while ago for a job in the US from a writer in India who extolled her immense talents and said that one of the things she was good at was "thinking outside box". It's a common enough expression, except that it isn't, because both in the UK and the US what you will hear is "thinking outside **the** box". I spent quite a bit of time in India when I was an international salesman and I know that leaving articles like "the" out of a sentence is common. That's true of a lot of countries because many languages – most, probably – change the word ending to mean that it's singular or plural, masculine or feminine and they don't have articles like "an" or "the", so people whose first language is not English often omit those words. "Thinking outside box" is a perfectly acceptable piece of Indian English but absolutely unacceptable as British English. Or American English. Or Australian, Canadian, South African or New Zealand English.

But that's what the client gets in return for a cut-price.

There's been a recent steady trend in British banks, retailers, computer manufacturers and others to repatriate Help Desks, which they had previously outsourced to the subcontinent, because the reduced costs did not offset the lost business when customers couldn't understand the Help Desk operative and the Help Desk operative couldn't understand the customers. I'm also aware of at least one prominent British SEO company that took its copywriting offshore and has now brought it back because, though they had employed the very best Indian writers they could find, their customers needed better copy and were going elsewhere in search of it. That process of bringing the work home is called "onshoring." Horrible word, but that's what people say.

I'm going to stress here that what I'm talking about is freelance writing. Nothing I've said should be taken as meaning that British graphics artists should also find a good freelance market because Photoshop and the other graphical tools are exactly the same in Sri Lanka as they are in the UK and the fact that practitioners in those two countries may speak different languages has no relevance to their ability to deliver an image that meets the customer's needs. Taking graphics work offshore is likely to last much longer than doing the same with writing work.

All right, so that's the obvious requirement out of the way – if you want to be a freelance writer, you have to be able to write, and write the kind of English that the customer wants. What else do you need?

Start with a willingness to work very hard

You need to be prepared to put in the hours every day, seven days a week. You're going out at nine on Wednesday and you'll be gone all day? That's fine – get up that day at four in the morning. Now you'll have time to get in your three hours, eat breakfast, take a shower and dress for your outing. Don't leave it till you get home because you'll be too tired.

In Chapter 3, I give an account of a typical seven day week during which I wrote 14,000 words of "my stuff" (in this case the latest rewrite of my current novel) and 35,250 words as a freelancer. Most writers don't get anywhere near that level of output, which is why most can only dream of paying the bills solely from their income from writing. (And I couldn't do it, either, if I didn't use voice recognition software – see below).

More recently, I've been able to cut the number of words I write as a freelancer because I've been working hard to push my rates up. It's an approach scorned by articles like the one I referred to when I talked about the writer who needed a new PC, but it worked for me and I see no reason why it shouldn't work for you.

Next, you have to rid yourself of fancy ideas about your writing

Novelists can be as precious as they like, but when the novelist switches to freelancing, s/he accepts that the required style is the one the client wants. Adopt this rule and make it yours:

> **The client is always right. Even when you're convinced the client is wrong, the client is right.**

Form a clear idea of your value as a freelancer and don't take less

If you read nothing else in this book, read this section.

A while ago, I was asked to "localise" a US website for the UK market (I have more to say about localising websites in Chapter 3). I looked at the website in question and decided how many hours it would take me to do the work. I already knew my hourly rate, so I multiplied one by the other and that's what I quoted. The prospective customer said they could get the job done in India for a fraction of my price. "Okay," I said, and left it.

How to Make Money as a Freelance Writer

Three weeks later, I got an email. It seemed the Indian writing team hadn't entirely understood what localising meant – they thought all they had to do was change some spellings. Did I still have time available to take on the project? I did it; since then I've done more work for that customer (without having to bid competitively for it) and I expect still more. The icing on the cake came when they gave my name to the marketing director at another company in the same American city and now I get work from that company, too.

They won't always come back to you (in fact, they'll come back less often than they don't) but the rule remains the same: know how much you're worth and don't work for less. I've already talked about the downward pressure on fees caused by people prepared to work for very little and in fact provided an extract from my PDF file, *Guide to Finding a Freelance Writer*. You can download the whole thing here: http://tinyurl.com/ngbjjmr, and although it's about how to find a writer rather than how to be one, it also contains information valuable to freelancers and will tell you a lot about how that downward pressure comes about.

Chapter 4 is about how to get business and I come back to the question of pricing then. For now, I'll just say that the best paying regular freelance job I have pays me six British pence a word (they don't all pay that; that's the best) which amounts to £72 (US$109) per hour. That calculation comes from the fact that it takes me fifty minutes on average to dictate, then proof read and then edit and check 1,000 words. As I've said before, if I didn't use voice recognition software (see below for more on that) I'd be doing a lot less well.

There are lots of people bidding for jobs on Upwork (more about Upwork in Chapter 4) who will quote US$5 per hour or even less, and Upwork will tell you with pride that a thousand new writers sign up with them every month. The doom mongers will say that that means you can't make a living as a freelancer. Well, no it doesn't – what it tells you is that the people prepared to work for US$5 per hour can't make what you would call a living. In my opinion, we are through the worst – enough customers have realised that many of those thousand new writers are in fact not "writers". They are not good enough.

That doesn't mean you should stay away from Upwork; there are some very fine writers on there and I'm one of them and 40% of my income currently comes that way. There are good reasons for doing business through Upwork. As I've said, I'll talk about that in Chapter 4.

Find repeat customers and make sure you give them what they want

Don't take a job on unless you're absolutely certain that you can meet the deadline. Then meet it. What you're looking for is people who have a high demand for good quality English writing and have already experienced the disappointment that comes from dealing with cut-price offshore providers. They know they have to pay to get what they want and, if you work at it hard enough, eventually they'll give you a trial. If you do a good job you'll get more work – if you don't, you'll never hear from them again.

I'll be talking in Chapter 3 about the various forms that freelance writing takes and in Chapter 4, I'll talk about how to find opportunities and how to sell yourself so that you get your share.

I'm in the UK, so why do I talk about dollars?

I talk about dollars because until recently most of my non-journalist work clients were not in the UK and the huge majority of my work was billed and paid for in dollars. As Tom Jones said, "it's not unusual"; it's true for most freelancers and it will almost certainly be true for you, at least at the beginning. I've focussed hard on getting more British customers and it's paying off.

Writing (and proofreading) good quality English

When I write a novel, it passes through various editing stages (typically, one of my novels will have three different editors), but the last thing that happens before it goes to the printer is that it is proofread. You need to distinguish between proofreaders and developmental editors. Let me give a practical example of what I mean by that. My coming-of-age novel, *Zappa's Mam's a Slapper*, had gone through five rewrites (fairly standard for me when I'm writing fiction) and close to the end of the process the editor had emailed me:

> John. I don't know how you're going to feel about this, but I have a problem with the last stage of the book. You've got Poppy chasing Billy and although I thought I was happy with it, I now feel it just doesn't work – you need Billy to be chasing Poppy.

I swore when I read that, because my first reaction was: "You must be joking. We've got 90,000 words, we're all agreed it's publishable and it's ready to go for proofreading. Now you want me to rip up the last 20,000 words and write another 20,000 to take their place. Are you out of your mind?"

But my second reaction was: "Of course. I knew something was wrong, but I couldn't put my finger on it. That's why we have editors." Then I worked like fury to replace the last 20,000 words and I knew as I went along that I was transforming the book into something much better.

That's developmental editing. You don't have time for that kind of work when you're freelancing and nor do you have the budget – you rely on the client to tell you if something doesn't meet her or his requirements and needs to be changed (and you change it – without argument. Remember what I said about not being precious?)

Most freelance writers will tell you they don't have the budget for proofreading, either.

They are probably right. And it's a pity. I believe you need to get a second pair of eyes to run through what you've written before it goes to the client. I accept, though, that most people aren't going to do that and so I ask you to master the proofreader's art and apply it to your own work.

One of the things you need to do that properly is a keen eye and you either have that or you don't. There are some other things you might find helpful, however. I can reach the following books without leaving the desk at which I work:

The Times Guide to English Style and Usage ISBN 0 7230 0544 3
The Economist Style Guide ISBN 0 09 174616 7
On Writing Well by William Zinsser (2nd Edition) ISBN 0 06 014804 7
New Oxford Style Manual ISBN 9 78 019965 7
The Copyeditor's Handbook ISBN 9 78 052027 1
The Cambridge Guide to English Usage ISBN 9 78 052162 816

I don't claim to have my nose in these all the time – they are reference books and I check things in them when I need to – but it is important to have an understanding of the basic rules. Since most of my work is in American English, if I had to get by with only one of these I would choose The Copyeditor's Handbook.

Developing a style
Before things reach the proofreading stage, there should be a dedicated effort always to write well. My first published book was *Managing the High-tech Salesforce* (ISBN 9 78185 058 1253). When a colleague read it, he said, "You write just like you speak." He said that as though I was somehow cheating and it left me a little miffed because I had

put an enormous amount of effort into developing a writing style that seemed to be writing the way I speak. In fact, of course, it was no such thing and nor should it be with you, because speech is filled with pauses, "ums", "ers" and the rest of what we go through as we assemble our thoughts. You'd never sell anything written like that.

I've headed this section "Developing a style" but "Developing styles" would have been more accurate. I've already said that I have at least half a dozen different styles and I was underestimating the number when I said that. My historical fiction is written in a different style from my contemporary fiction which, itself, varies according to whether I'm writing in the first or third person. I produce regular blog posts for no fewer than 16 different US companies and they want different things – some are chatty posts resembling a conversation you might have with the person in the next seat at a baseball game and some are posts with the height of formality.

It's a mistake to try to copy someone else's style. What you need to work on is something that reflects you but is also acceptable to your client.

Keyboard or voice recognition software?

Clearly, this has to be each individual's choice, but I could not be as prolific as I am (you'll see a list of a typical week's work at the beginning of Chapter 3) without Dragon voice recognition software. I tried it when it first came out years ago and it was hopeless – it didn't recognise a word I said. In 2014, I was told that it had improved and I had enough respect for the person who said that to try it again. She was right. There was no comparison between the early effort I had first tried out and what we now have. I know, though, that I'm someone who finds talking easier than typing (just ask someone who knows me) and I can write three or four times the number of words in a given time if I can speak the first draft instead of using a keyboard. If you're like that and you haven't tried Dragon, I recommend it.

Why make the effort to be a freelance writer?

Because, in the famous (and possibly apocryphal) words of American bank robber Willie Sutton, "That's where the money is." Writing fiction is a lottery. Some very good writers are extremely well paid. Others who are just as good earn nothing at all. Most are in between, but if the majority of people setting out today to become novelists knew what the average income from writing novels was, the only people to undertake it would be people like me who have to write, whether we earn any money from it or not.

Freelancing can produce a regular income that is enough to keep a roof over your head, put food on the table and send your children to school. Most novelists can only achieve those aims by having a regular job and restricting their fiction writing to evenings and weekends.

As a freelancer, you won't be famous. No-one will invite you to literary parties or book launches. More often than not, your name won't appear on the piece you wrote. But you will know you wrote it, you can tell your friends – and you'll get paid.

Not everyone will want to pay you. There are extremely successful and profitable blogs and one day, if you have enough work posted, you're likely to get an invitation to let them post something of yours. You will be told there's no fee but you'll have a byline and the blog is so widely read that appearing there cannot help but bring you goodwill and boost your career. What you do about that invitation must remain your choice, but my advice is that you do what I do and tell them that your supermarket, perhaps unlike theirs, doesn't accept goodwill at the checkout and if they don't pay, they don't publish.

Copyscape

If you haven't heard of Copyscape, you'll find it here: http://www.copyscape.com/; it enables people to check whether a piece of work submitted to them is actually plagiarism – that is, the "writer" has either reproduced whole chunks of someone else's work or has cannibalised it in a way that still leaves it clear that the rewritten article is an act of theft. Copyscape will check a document against content on the whole of the Web or against another document.

Copyscape is widely used and you should expect anyone to whom you submit blog posts, news articles or a host of other things to check whether what you are sending is really all your own work or has been stolen in whole or in part from another writer. As a writer yourself, I hope you share my view that copyright is to be respected and plagiarism is even more evil than broccoli. (I ate broccoli for years for a quiet life before I thought, "Why am I doing this? I hate the stuff." That was ten years ago and I haven't touched it since). But if you don't share my view (of copyright and plagiarism; I don't really mind how you feel about broccoli. Someone has to eat it), then be aware that a plagiarist is likely to be found out before their piece is published and won't be paid. They may also be blacklisted. Bloggers and publishers talk to each other. If they talk about you, you want them saying good things and not accusing you of stealing other people's work.

Titles

Writing a good title is an art and it's one the freelancer needs to master. I have a regular client who would smile if she read that because she has corrected my titles a number of times. Too often, I treat the title as an afterthought and that's a common freelance mistake. You need to deal with it, just as I have. Very often what happens is that the writer puts time into doing the best possible job on the written piece itself and then dashes off the title in a couple of minutes. If you Google "How to write a good title" you'll find all sorts of web pages with suggestions you may find useful. When you're trying to sell a piece on spec to someone you've never worked for before (see Chapter 4), the title may be the thing that makes the sale.

Chapter 3

What kind of work is there for freelancers?

I said in Chapter 2 that there was plenty of work for freelancers. I don't pretend that the list I'm about to give includes everything, but it should provide a good introduction; certainly everything I do is included here. I've just been through my records (I keep spreadsheets for this purpose because if there's one thing a freelancer must be it's organised) and I extracted this list of my freelance work load from the final week in 2015:

- localised 11 pages from a US company's website for their UK site
- wrote from scratch the content for two new websites, each of nine pages
- 19 blog posts for a total of nine different companies
- 19 news articles for events that had happened within the previous 24 hours
- four posts for blogs, which I maintain on behalf of the owners
- one chapter of a ghostwritten autobiography
- two selling items for products about to come to market

Normally there would also have been at least one article sold to a trade magazine but that didn't happen in that week. The impression I had was that most of the trade magazine editors had cleared off for the holiday. The above work amounted to 35,250 words in seven days and, in addition to those 35,250 words, I wrote 14,000 words of the fifth rewrite of my current novel (*When the Darkness Comes*). See Chapter 2 for my comments on hard work; here I'll say only that, like most writers, I couldn't even think of writing that many words a week of fiction. Freelance writing feels different and it *is* different.

Since I put my minimum rates up and cut the number of freelance words I was prepared to write in a week, that total word count has come down but the income has stayed the same. That can happen for you, too. But you have to get there first. You have to write what it takes to convince enough of the higher paying clients that you are the writer they want to use regularly. You have to work hard and you have to be good.

I'll now go through the different requirements of each of the different types of freelance work listed above.

Localising US pages for the UK and vice versa

This has become one of my most remunerative areas of work. There's a fundamental misunderstanding among many people about exactly what localising is and the question is best approached by saying what it is not; localising is not simply a matter of changing spellings (like altering "localising" to "localizing" in this sentence).

Oscar Wilde, George Bernard Shaw and Winston Churchill have all been credited with describing the US and the UK as "two countries divided by a common tongue". Whoever first said it, there's more to it than just the language. Americans and the British don't just speak differently, they think differently and you can't transfer a website from one culture to the other without understanding that.

I've already described how I came to do one localising job when an Indian company had failed to deliver what was needed. I lived in North America for a number of years and I think that's a great help to anyone who wants to do this kind of – this kind of what? I hesitate to call it "translation", though I'd find it difficult to come up with a more accurate word. Watching Hollywood movies and reading Elmore Leonard is not enough (though, if you like crime fiction and you're not familiar with Elmore Leonard's work, I recommend it in the strongest possible terms). A decent spellchecker will tell you where the spelling differences are, but it takes more than that. The very least you need is an understanding of the idiomatic differences and, even more so, what certain concepts mean in the two countries. To give a simple example, in the pages I localised last week, the company spoke of "reaching out" to its customers. That would be a perfectly reasonable expression to use in the US, but I removed it from the UK pages because too many British businessmen would want nothing to do with a company that spoke of "reaching out" to them.

As well as everything else you do need to know that Americans say "a couple eggs" whereas the British would put "of" between "couple" and "eggs". And it's fine in the US but not in the UK to say "I took this off of…" And…well. The list isn't endless but it is very long. If you're going to take on localisation jobs, you need to know most of the things on that list.

When she reached this point in the book, my editor (Kirstie Edwards, since you ask; I recommend her wholeheartedly and you can find her here: http://www.kirstieedwards.eu/) said "Can you point to any references or sources to help your readers learn these differences?" And I looked – quite hard – and the fact is that I can't. We all know the song "I say tomato, You say tomato" and it's true that Americans don't pronounce that word correctly, just as it's true that they all drive on the wrong side of the road; it's also true that whoever wrote it seems to think there's also a difference in the way we say "potato" which, of course, there isn't. But when I tried to find serious articles about the difference in word choice, construction and grammar, they weren't there. There were lots of jokey web pages, but nothing that's any use. If you're going to be serious about localisation work, you need to have lived in both countries.

You also need to be ready to do research and to do it effectively. Very recently, I was asked to localise a page that began like this:

> In 2014, Equipment World released results from a survey conducted by the Associated General Contractors of America. The survey found that from more than 1,000 construction firms across the US, 83% reported that they're struggling to find enough craft workers. That percentage is up from 74% just one year prior. Of those same firms surveyed, 61 percent said they're having trouble filling professional positions, which includes project surveyors, estimators, and engineers. That number I also up from 53 percent one year ago.

Of course, the immediate problem with this is that it deals with an American magazine describing an American Association conducting a survey on problems faced by American companies. The blog post is intended to tell visitors that the company whose blog it is understands the environment they work in, and this post was to go into a British blog with British visitors. Would they be impressed to be told how things were in America?

I didn't think so. And so I rewrote the post, starting with this:

> The Annual Manufacturing Report for 2016 had some worrying things to say about the developing skills shortage:
>
> UK manufacturing needs more skilled workers
> - 84% of respondents said they have multiple vacancies and
> - 22% said that they have 10 or more.

Now, UK visitors can see that this post has something to say to them. Oddly enough, I don't carry around in my head details of manufacturing reports – for the UK, for the US or for anywhere else. So the first thing I had to do was to find a source of information that I could substitute for what was in the original American post. If you want to make a success of localising American websites and blogs for the UK market (by success I mean that you get invited to do it again. And again), you have to be prepared to do that kind of research. Examine every element of the page or post you are looking at, decide which are not appropriate for the translation to UK English, and find something to put in their place. Once the customer knows they can rely on you they will want to use you again. They may also recommend you to other people and they'll almost certainly be prepared to speak for you if a potential client asks for a reference.

This:

> I don't know whether this will be necessary in the States, but I do think that for a lot of people in this country, and particularly those who are not I specialists, we need to explain what a native app is and why it doesn't matter if there's no wireless signal. So I've done that.

is an example of the sort of comment I give when I'm explaining what I'm doing and this is another:

> The first paragraph is fine, except that the fact that something is made for today's mobile environment does not automatically make it easy to use. The second paragraph has some faults that I suggest you need to change on the US site as well as this one. In the first place, the word "unique" appears three times and that is two times too many. Also, remove the grocer's apostrophe in "tablet's". Because "applications" is plural, "takes" should not have the s on the end. Finally, there is no space between "and" and "or". You don't need to say "some of" if you then say "include" – include implies some of.
>
> The first bullet point says, 'i.e. Siri...' I.e. is an abbreviation of id est, Latin for "that is" and is to be distinguished from "e.g." which means "for example". So the question is, are Siri, maps and photo gallery the only pre-installed applications? If they are, then the bullet is right as it stands but if not then e.g. should be substituted.

> The second bullet point is "Processing power" and I suggest that that is not unique to ▮▮▮▮. Yours may be the most powerful implementation of processing power but it is not the only one. However, once we remove the word unique, that ceases to matter. You don't need to deliver information "out" to the field worker.

Both of those were from work I did for a B2B software company.

PDF files are popular as downloads from websites and, if you're engaged in localising websites, sooner or later you will be asked to do the same with a PDF. I've done several of these; the localisation is straightforward and follows the same rules as for web pages and blog posts but you will be a lot more popular if the PDF you return to the client is exactly the same in layout and all aspects of formatting as the one you received. Adobe Acrobat DC is the best way to do this because it is set up to allow more than one user to comment on and modify PDF files.

Take a close look at any Web links. Do you need to modify them to refer to a UK site instead of an American site? That is, to a site ending in .uk rather than in .com? If so, don't stop there; right click on the link after you changed it, then click on "Edit Link" and type the URL of the UK site to replace the US URL.

Writing websites and blog posts
SEO

Writing a complete website from scratch and writing a blog post are two different things and I'll deal with them separately. One thing is common to both, though, and that is SEO. I've already talked about what those letters mean; if SEO is a closed book to you, there are some things you need to master before you get started on people's websites and blog posts. I recommend *SEO for WordPress* by Kent Mauresmo, simply because more than a quarter of the world's blogs use WordPress and many of the things that count there count everywhere else, too. Pay particular attention to what he has to say about keywords and anchor text because, if you're not bearing those in mind when you write, you're going to have some unhappy customers.

Because knowledgeable SEO people are beginning to talk about conversion optimisation as frequently as they do about SEO, you could do worse than follow Kent Mauresmo's book with Master the Essentials of Conversion Optimisation by Peep Laja. It's a more challenging read than SEO for WordPress, but it will repay the effort and at least, when you talk to potential customers, they will have the comforting feeling that you speak the same language. If you mention the book to one of those potential clients, remember that "Peep" is pronounced "Pep" or the idea that you're steeped in the subject may not take hold.

I'm going to talk in Chapter 5 about how things change and I'll have something then to say about SEO and how I think web page and blog post writers need to change if they are to continue to be successful. I warn you now: most of the experts in the field disagree with me. They are wrong.

Bear in mind (and I've mentioned this elsewhere) that SEO is not only, as some people seem to think, a matter of keywords. I'm not going to say more about this here, because this is not a specialist book about SEO, but you need to get into this and understand it.

Read the brief

Of course that sounds obvious; of course you'll read the brief. I know. I always read the brief, too. But sometimes, even though I've read it, I fail to do everything I've been asked to do. Here's an example. This was the brief:

> Write two paragraphs about the "Foot in the door" online marketing technique. Show how it can help in lead generation.

How difficult could that be? Not difficult at all if you happen to have the background and knowledge base that I have; you take on fiddling little jobs like this because the client is someone who uses you a lot and you want to keep them happy. I knocked it off in about eight minutes. This is what I wrote:

> The Foot in the Door Marketing Technique
>
> Not many of us would react kindly to a salesperson who came to our door and then stuck a foot inside to prevent us closing it. But that's not what "Foot in the Door Marketing" is about. Foot in the Door is a way to make a positive answer to a large request a great deal more likely by making a small request first.
>
> For example, what you really want is someone's commitment to take your online photography course. You start with a seemingly harmless request for their comment on a simple proposition: perhaps which of two pictures is better composed. Immediately they've clicked

> on one of the pictures (either; it really doesn't matter which they choose) present them with another choice, this time of three simple and well-known photographic "rules" (like the Rule of Thirds) and ask them which of these they've heard of. The third screen is the one that asks them to sign up to your course and studies have shown clearly that you are MUCH more likely to get a "Yes" to the third and big request having already had a positive response to the two smaller ones.

That's all right, isn't it? Fits the bill, doesn't it?

Well, no. It isn't and it doesn't. Where's the bit about lead generation?

As I said, read the brief. Your client will almost certainly come back and point out to you that you're missing something, giving you the chance to fix it, but you don't want that. What you want is to get a reputation as someone who meets the brief spot on, every time. A magazine editor once told me I was an editor's dream. That is exactly what you want to aim for. Fortunately, before I sent this one off, I re-read it and noticed that I hadn't completed the job I had been asked to do.

Research the subject

To write this section, I did a quick scan through the record I keep of work done. These are some of the blog posts I wrote over a two-day period:

- Asian influences on California home decor
- the impact of the FDA's 2017 deadline on the American prescription drug supply chain
- the discovery of a bronze age wheel in the Cambridgeshire fens
- Valle de Guadalupe winery tours in summer
- how to make a "constructed photograph"
- changes and continuity in furniture materials

That's quite a range of subject matter and, if you look back at what I said my particular skills were, there's really no match at all. Preparing a list of the things you know about and the things that you're good at will help you launch your first attack on the market but once you're established as a content writer and you have clients who use you regularly you write about what you are asked to write about. As it happens, I've become something of an expert on the American prescription drug supply chain (and a fascinating world it is ☺) and I do know something about photography but the other subjects are as much a closed book to me as they may be to you. So what did I do when asked to write about them? I researched.

We are lucky in the volume of material available on the Web and research is a lot easier than it would once have been but:

- don't forget that an enormous amount of information on the Internet is wrong. It was put there by people who didn't know what they were talking about, had a political or personal axe to grind, were deluded (sometimes beyond the point of insanity) or just wanted to cause trouble. So check it. You're a writer, so always use what Hemingway said was the writer's essential tool: a built-in bullshit detector.
- don't simply rewrite and regurgitate what you find. Remember Copyscape; even if you don't use it yourself, you'd better assume that your client does. If you want to build a reputation and have clients knocking on your door asking you to write for them, everything you write needs to be a fresh view and presented in an appealing way. Yes, even when you're writing about the prescription drug supply chain.

This is such a vital part of the freelance writer's armoury that I'm going to spend some time talking about how to improve your search techniques. The first rule is: think very hard about exactly what it is you want to know. That will tell you how to write the search engine queries. So, for example, let's say I am asked to write a blog post on *Is Medium a Suitable Platform For You?* Writing about online marketing is supposed to be one of my specialities so I'm certainly not going to admit to the client that I don't really know anything about Medium. I need to get some information – but here's the thing; I need to get it quickly because, if I spend a long time researching an article and I only get paid for what I write and not for the research I do then I'm going to shoot holes in my carefully constructed pricing model.

Right. First thing: what *is* Medium? That's easy enough; just search for "Medium."

We get the first hint that it might not be quite as easy as that when Google (because that's the search engine I'm using, and I mentioned this to remind you that Google is not the only search engine) offers to search for: "Medium length hair hairstyles," "Medium dog breeds," and "Medium brown hair." It's alright, though, because when I hit the Enter key the first thing I see after a paid advertisement for a psychic is the website www.Medium.com. The description says that "it's a community of readers and writers offering unique perspectives on ideas large and small." That sounds as though it could be what I've been asked to write about so I'll click on it. (If that hadn't worked, I'd have looked again at the title of the blog post I've been asked to write and

I'd probably have searched for "Medium AND platform." The AND tells the search engine that I want results that contain both of those words).

The Medium website turns out to be one of those that invite you to get started right away and all I want to do is find out about it. Fortunately, there's also a button that says "Learn More" and that's the one I click. If that had not been there, I'd have gone straight on to the review search I'm going to write about in a minute or two.

I start reading what the Medium people say about their product and I'm hooked almost straight away by this:

> ### Read Actively
> Stories that mean something
> The world has reached a saturation point of shallow, thoughtless content, and half-skimming through these pages of filler is increasingly unfulfilling

"The world has reached a saturation point of shallow, thoughtless content." Well, substitute "The Web" for "The world" and you can say that again! This is one of my central preoccupations right now and I cover it in Chapter 5. I wrote a blog post a while ago for one of my clients with the title, "If you're writing what everyone else is writing, what on earth is the point?" Far too much of what is posted online every day is either rubbish, or says what a hundred thousand other people have already said, or is rubbish that says what a hundred thousand other people have already said. If blogging is to continue to have any point, someone has to put an end to this and the someone will need to be us – the quality writers in a sea of incompetents. And, yes, I do know that sounds arrogant. I'll say when I talk about ghostwriting that I don't know too many writers who lack ego and I'm not one of them. The "us" I'm talking about is the body of writers good enough for clients to be prepared to pay them forty, fifty or sixty pounds an hour and come back again and again because they are getting the quality they want.

Enough of that; I go through the rest of the Medium website and now I know enough about the Medium platform to be able to introduce the blog post, but what I'd been asked to write about is *"Is Medium a Suitable Platform For You?"* and I'm not going to find the answer to that solely by reading the platform's own website, because they are bound to tell me that it's a suitable platform for anyone. I need to know what other people think.

So now I do a new search: "Medium writing platform reviews." (I write it like that and not just "Medium reviews" because I don't want to find myself submerged in reviews of people who read tarot cards for a living, or produce reams of butter muslin from their mouths). This produces a number of hits but one is a paid advertisement and one will take me back to the Medium site so I focus on these three:

> What's With New Blogging Platforms Like Medium?
>
> Is it a good idea to write articles on Medium versus another…
>
> A Platform and Blogging Tool, Medium Charms Writers

These three give me enough information to write my piece. Which is what I now do.

I'm writing this piece for an agency so when I've finished I hit the Enter key a few times to give a little space and then type the underlined word "SOURCES." Under that, I'll put the URL of every site for which I took information for my post. That's what agencies expect, and you should do the same.

That was a fairly easy bit of searching to get the material for the post I'd been asked to write. It isn't always that simple and content writers need to become expert in search techniques. Rather than simply filling up a few pages with stuff you can learn elsewhere, I searched "How to improve online search techniques" and got some promising hits. You should do the same and then spend time really mastering all the ins and outs of searching. Most people don't do this; if you do it will pay off for you. Pay particular attention to use of the words AND, OR and NOT and symbols like the ~. They can make you a much more efficient content writer.

Style

Whether you're writing a single post or a whole website, you need a clear understanding of the style the site owner is aiming at. I've already said that last week I wrote 19 blog posts for nine different companies. I'd written for all of them before and they expect that the style of any new post I send them will match the style of previous posts which, in turn, will have matched the "house style". The house style of each of the nine companies is different (as you might expect; one of them is a law firm, two are software companies, two more are employment agencies, and so on). None of them would be happy if they got a post in a style that wasn't theirs. A professional would not make that mistake – and you're going to be a professional, so you won't make it.

Keywords and Calls to Action

The first time you are asked to write a post, ask the client these questions:

1. What are the keywords for the website as a whole, and what are they for this post? (Be prepared to be asked for advice; the Mauresmo book will come in handy if you don't know how to find keywords. The Google Keyword Planner Tool is useful and you can find it by logging into Gmail and going to http://adwords.google.com/keywordplanner, but the most useful keyword finder in my view is Keyword Optimizer Pro which can be downloaded from http://www.keywordoptimizerpro.com/.)
2. Which existing posts most capture the style they regard as theirs?
3. With what kind of CTA (Call To Action) do they like to end their posts? (Usually, this will be something that encourages the reader to make contact, ask a question, buy a product or otherwise meet the commercial purpose of the website, but I do write for one client who doesn't like any kind of hard CTA; all they want is a question that asks something like "What do you do in these circumstances?"
4. What do they see as the ideal number of words?

More About Style

When you have answers to the second question, look at those posts with great care. They should embody the house style that you need to be copying. First, ask yourself what the writing style is: friendly, distant, professional, jokey, casual, factual – there are so many different styles. Get clear in your mind what this client wants. Then look at the way the information is organised. How long are a typical sentence and a typical paragraph? Are there subheadings? If so, how are they formatted and what sort of thing do they say? Look at the CTA. Does how it's written match their response to question three?

When you write blog posts, expect as a matter of course that the client will make changes. Sometimes – if you're like me – you'll look at the changes and think, "Yes, I see the reason for that and I agree it improves the piece." Other times, you'll think, "I don't think there was any need to make that change, but if that's what you want…" And sometimes your reaction will be, "I'm sorry, Client, but you're wrong. That change is not only unnecessary, it's also a retrograde step – it reduces the quality of the post."

Remember what I said in Chapter 2 about not being precious about your writing? If an editor of one of your novels wants to make changes that you really disagree with, you'll stand your ground and argue your point. When it's a piece you submitted as a writer for hire, you don't do that. Recently I wrote a post for a marketing company and they came back to me on Friday afternoon to say that their client did not like the way I used parentheses and would also like a couple of other changes in emphasis and could I possibly rewrite the piece in time for Monday morning? (That's even easier in their case than it might have been because both marketing company and client are on the American east coast so their morning is my afternoon). I said yes, of course I could, no problem and I got a reply telling me what a wonderful person I am to work with and how so many writers this agency uses throw a tantrum when asked to change something.

Now, I could have given a very honest reply along these lines: "Two men tried to kidnap me in Lagos, Nigeria. I was actually in the Corinthia Hotel in Tripoli, Libya when an armed and hostile militia came in to take the Prime Minister away. I was standing outside that same hotel talking to someone when a car bomb exploded. I was 20 minutes from touching down at Erbil Airport in northern Iraq when we had to turn back to Vienna because the place where we wanted to land was being shelled. I had to remonstrate with some extremely agitated demonstrators in Bahrain because they were interfering with the job I was doing. And some guy doesn't like the way I use parentheses? Well, whooptido."

But I didn't. What in fact I wrote was:

"What can I say? Well – this:

Rule One:
> The client is always right.

Rule Two:
> When the client is wrong, refer to Rule One."

Her reply? "Words to live by when dealing with clients."

And they are. Don't forget them. If, though, your name is appearing on the piece, you have the right to explain that you have made the change but you don't approve of it (and give the reasons) and ask for your name to be removed before publication.

I don't think a week goes by when I don't have all four of those reactions (I agree, I'll revise; this is unnecessary but I'll revise; I don't agree and I'll justify why, or I don't agree but if you insist on revising I don't want my name on it) to changes made by clients. Sometimes the client is right; sometimes the client is neither right nor wrong, but it really doesn't matter; and sometimes the client is wrong but I keep my mouth shut and don't argue the point.

Before we move on from blog posts, let's talk about quotations and images, because a quotation can be a good way to begin a business-oriented post and images are really essential.

Quotations

A quotation is often a good way to introduce a post. (I said often – not always. To begin every post you write for a particular site in exactly the same way will be boring and writing a boring post is possibly the single worst thing you can do because you turn visitors away and the chances are they never come back).

Quotations are easy to find. You probably already know some of them yourself. Some time before midday tomorrow, I am contracted to write a blog post about how rapidly the writer's job changes (see Chapter 5) and how what worked very well a few months ago may not work today. TS Eliot said:

> "one has only learnt to get the better of words
>
> For the thing one no longer has to say, or the way in which
>
> One is no longer disposed to say it"

and, in planning that post, I had considered beginning with those words. In fact, I've decided instead on another Eliot quote: "For last year's words belong to last year's language" because it's shorter and still apposite.

Now, as it happens, I didn't have to look either of those quotations up because, thanks partly to a good memory but mainly to an inspiring sixth form English teacher of 55 years ago, I carry around huge chunks of Eliot, Auden, Spender and a number of other poets and they swim into my head when required. If, though, I can't think of the quote I need, I go to a site like http://www.quotationspage.com/ or http://www.quotationreference.com/, insert the subject and see what comes up.

(And, even when I do remember the quote I want to use, I still double check it to make sure I've got it precisely right).

Images

In the case of images, what I said about not starting every post the same way probably doesn't apply. It's a good rule to assume that, unless there's a very good reason not to include an image, every post should have one. Visitors like images and will often click on them.

When you're writing for someone else's blog, this won't usually be a matter for you. The blog owner will find an image to go with your post. Larger companies will usually have their own stock image library. There will be times, though, when the blog owner asks you to provide the image and of course you will want to do that. So be aware that there can be problems of copyright with images. You're a writer and you wouldn't dream of breaking someone else's copyright, now would you? You know how furious you'd be if you saw someone infringing yours and that alone would be enough to prevent you from doing it to somebody else. Am I right? I really hope I am; I could not express any warmth for a writer who did not have sufficient regard for the copyright of others.

If you do decide to use an image that isn't yours, you may find yourself in trouble because a lot of images that you find online have software embedded in them to say, in effect, "This image is copyright Joe Bloggs" and Joe Bloggs may very well have software of his own that searches the Web looking for his images being used by someone else. If that happens, the someone else should expect to receive a lawyer's letter demanding a large amount of money.

The big picture libraries (like Getty Images) enforce their copyright vigorously and so they should because the fee they charge is shared with the photographer who is often, like you, a freelancer. If you really like one of their images and can't find something else that would do as well, find out what the charge would be and ask the blog owner if they want to pay for it.

It isn't, however, the well-known big names like Getty that you need to watch out for. There are people who go to a great deal of trouble to have their images picked up, just so that they can sue. Rather than go into detail that you can read elsewhere, I'll invite you to click on this link for a sobering story:

 http://www.livingfornaptime.com/starting-a-blog/blogging-mistakes-to-avoid/.

There are places you can download images from for a very small fee. (They will frequently use words like "free images" but the images are very rarely totally without charge). It's in the nature of things, though, that their images are not usually as good as the ones on the big Getty and Adobe sites.

Writing a complete website

There are two occasions when I write a complete website. The first is when someone is going online for the first time – usually it will be a new business because the number of ongoing businesses that still don't have a website is now very small – and the second is something else, which I'll explain in a minute.

Even when you're dealing with a new business, it's unlikely that the business owner has no previous experience with websites and no idea of what they want. And remember: what we're discussing here is the writer's job – the content. If you're also taking on design of the website then that's very exciting, but it's beyond the scope of this book, so I'm going to assume that someone else is responsible for the overall layout.

Let me make it clear that I'm only making this assumption for the purpose of this book. It may be that, after you've written the content, someone else will put it online and that is the case for me with a number of the blogs I write for, because my client in those cases is not the blogger but a firm that deals with bloggers (see Chapter 4). That firm employs mostly freelancers (like me) and one of the freelancers is the person who puts the posts online. I do, though, have a client who wants my stuff in HTML and I have other clients – including the four websites I maintain – where, having written the posts, I put my blogging hat on and post them online. Anyone who wants to be serious about developing a freelance career involving blog posts has to be capable of going all the way through to the final stage of uploading what they have written. That's a fact but it's also outside the scope of this book.

Even if you're not the person uploading the finished product, you will often need to insert hyperlinks. I have one client for whom I write regularly who likes to have half a dozen hyperlinks scattered among 500 words. Because I write in Microsoft Word and send my pages and posts as docx files (except to the client who wants HTML), I can insert hyperlinks and know that they will still be there when the client receives them, but if you're posting online yourself you'll need to check to make sure the links have carried over – and, if they haven't, insert them manually.

In any case, you will begin with some questions very similar to the ones in the previous section, because what you want to know is: what kind of style and what kind of material does this customer want to have? Ask the customer for examples of websites they particularly like as well as websites they really don't, and get into the CTA question again. What is the overall objective of this website? (To make a sale on the first visit? To get someone to ask for a quotation? To arrange a visit?) How can each page and each post most effectively lead visitors to do what the website owner wants them to do? And ask the question about keywords, because if you don't pay attention to keywords, the website's SEO will never be satisfactory and the site may as well not exist.

It's a good idea to send drafts as you go along, especially in the early days, to make sure that you don't do too much work heading in a direction other than the one the client wants.

I said there was a second case in which I write complete websites and I do two or three of these a week. I have a client, part of whose business is to find buyers for websites that existed in the past, but that have been allowed to expire. (There are good SEO reasons for buying such a site, as long as it existed for a while in its previous incarnation and a lot of people linked to it). Many agents buying such websites charge money to get the name reassigned to the new owner. However, there is really no point in the new website buyers paying the fee, because you can do it yourself by contacting Internet Corporation for Assigned Names and Numbers (ICANN: www.icann.org) and handing over $10. What my client does, though, is to add value by buying the name, creating a completely new website and selling the whole as a going concern. Writing the content for those websites is where I come in.

If you find yourself with an assignment like that, you'll have the keywords pointed out to you, but questions of style are usually much more straightforward. In any case, this particular client is very experienced and tells me before I start exactly what I'm required to do. That's an advantage with any client – I wish they were all like that.

News articles

As I said, last week I wrote 19 of these and I wrote them all for the same client. I'm one of a number of freelancers that client uses. The place where the articles appear looks like a news site, but in fact the news items are only there to get visitors onto the site so they can look at the advertisements for goods and services for sale. (I also write some of those advertisements).

When we began, the client would send me details of the articles they would like me to write that day. The details were frequently simply a URL and what was being proposed was a rewrite of someone else's article. I'll cover rewriting in a minute, because it's a big area for freelancers. As it happens, I don't like rewrites because they strike me as something very close to plagiarism. That was one of two reasons I had for disliking the approach the client took; the other was that I had no control over the amount of material I would be asked for. If they wanted one article, that's what I'd do; if they asked for five, I'd do that. So I took matters in hand and began every evening to send them four or five headlines for articles I'd be happy to write the following day. I made it clear these were just suggestions; they could have an article on anything they wanted. For the last little while, they've responded by asking for all of the articles on my list and I have become the biggest single contributor to that website.

I make my list by searching through RSS feeds from a wide variety of sources as well as looking at a number of newspapers around the world for which I have a high regard and checking out the Google News pages for a number of countries. I try to

make sure that what I'm offering represents a wide range of subject matter. For example, the headlines I sent yesterday (and I ended up writing all of these) were:
- Highlights from the Consumer Electronics Show
- Venezuela opposition swears in lawmakers barred by Supreme Court
- Bahrain says it has dismantled a terror cell linked to Iran
- Ghana makes room for two Yemenis held in Guantanamo for 14 years without charge

Today's (and, once again, I have written them all) were:
- Libya truck bomb attack on police base kills at least 60
- What Bill Clinton really thought about other world leaders (and Gaddafi thought of Tony Blair)
- Confusion in Nigeria as source of election funding is uncovered
- Iraqi forces start on the road to Mosul with special forces raids

If you can get a client to allow you the same freedom to choose what you write about, you'll be a happier writer because you'll be writing something that interests you, but don't expect that as a matter of course. You're a freelancer – a writer for hire – and you write about what you're hired to write about. You also write in the way that you're hired to write because:

It's Not (necessarily) a Soapbox

As anyone who knows me would tell you, I have quite strong political opinions. I have no idea how strong the opinions are of the people who own the website I write news articles for, or in which direction they lean. I don't know because they haven't told me. What I can be sure of is that the people who read my articles on the website don't know what my opinions are. I'm writing news. It has become clear that the site owners have complete confidence in what I write and don't even check it any more before putting it online. (They are the people who take my stuff in HTML). That's nice to know, but it is not carte blanche to express a view. If you are hired to write news articles, assume that you are being asked to say what happened and not what you think about it.

It's possible, of course, that the site owners may tell you what slant they want you to take and there may be times when that means you have to turn business down. I'll be frank enough about my own opinions here to say that, if the Leave.EU campaign asked me to write for them, I would do so and I wouldn't charge them, whereas there isn't enough money in the world to get me to write an article in favour of the UK staying in the EU. That doesn't mean that I'm free to express my own opinion on someone else's website.

But note the word "necessarily" in the heading two paragraphs ago. I do have a client who leaves me absolutely free to write anything I want in any way I choose. And I take full advantage of it. I write the articles I want to write with the slant I want to give them. Sometimes, the articles attract a lot of comments and some of the comments aren't good. My client just smiles and says, 'Write another one just like that,' because what we have done is increase the "conversation rate" and that is good.

(If you never heard the expression "conversation rate," no, I'm not making a mistake, really meaning to write "conversion rate." The conversation rate is the number of comments a piece gets and sensible blog owners know that the more comments, the better. It's good SEO, because although no one really knows all the ins and outs of the algorithms used by the main search engines, it's pretty certain that they are influenced by the number of comments). I'll come back to this in Chapter 5.

Plagiarism

What I'm going to say now is my opinion and may not be yours. I won't take a news item published by someone else and simply reword it, because I'm a writer and I have a clear view on copyright and plagiarism. That's why I tend to look at RSS feeds and press statements coming from government ministries, scientific establishments, PR departments and so forth more than newspapers – though I do look at those, too, because they can be a good source of ideas. I look at feeds and press statements with, I suppose, a fairly jaundiced eye and I try to get independent views.

Very, very occasionally, instead of obtaining an independent quote I will make one up but the circumstances in which I do so are very limited. Here is an example:

Black tarantula is named Johnny Cash. Reincarnation?

Published: February 06, 2016

There's a new tarantula on the block. It's dressed entirely in black. And it was found in Folsom, California – home of the penitentiary where the late, great Johnny Cash sang to the convicts. Dressed in black? Folsom Prison? Well – what would you have called it?

The researchers at Auburn University and Millsaps College had no doubt. They have named the eight legged creature Aphonopelma johnnycashi.

Chris Hamilton, author of a study in the journal ZooKeys, admits that he is "a huge Johnny Cash fan. But I didn't go into this searching for something I could name after him."

Hamilton is cautious, though, about the question other Johnny Cash fans are asking. 'Is this Johnny reincarnated? I don't know. I really can't say. We haven't heard him sing yet.'

I'm not going to lie to you – Chris Hamilton did not speak those last four sentences. I put the words into his mouth because I thought they made a nice, humorous addition to a very lightweight story. The day I wrote that piece, I also wrote eight hundred words for the same client on the subject of the failure of the Syrian peace talks in Geneva. I didn't make up any quotes for that piece, or put words into anyone's mouth. To do that would have been completely wrong. I hope you see the difference.

Note written later. When she saw what I've written there, my editor said: '"You realise there's a risk people will read that and say, "John Lynch says it's all right to put things in people's mouths."' I don't say that. Except in the absolute lightest of circumstances like the one above, it is never alright to say that someone said something they didn't say. Never.

Ghostwriting

Ghostwriting means that you write something that someone else will publish as though they had written it themselves. In that sense, it's not unlike the academic writing I mention later in this chapter (as something I don't do), but ghostwriting

usually involves someone's autobiography. Ghostwritten autobiographies can be divided into two groups:
- those you write as part of a direct contract between you and the "author" (author in inverted commas because the actual author is you, but that's not what it will say on the cover); *and*
- those where your client is a publisher who has agreed to publish the "author's" story and then contracted you to be the person who actually writes it.

In the latter case, the contract you sign will be drawn up by the publisher and will tell you what you are to do. This may be restricted to questions of formatting, number of chapters and number of words or may have something to say about style. (Even if that isn't actually in the contract, the publisher will certainly speak to you about the way they want the book to read, aspects of the person's life that must be included and – sometimes – events in that life that they would prefer not to be mentioned). If this book is going to be sold and is not just something for the "author" to give to his or her family, then when you think of style, remember what the doyen of ghostwriting, Christy Walsh, said. "A new ghostwriter usually makes the mistake of thinking he ought to write the way his celebrity speaks. That is an error. He ought to write the way the public thinks his celebrity speaks."

Which brings me to the other way ghostwritten autobiographies can be divided:
- those that are wanted by a regular publisher and where the "author" is a celebrity whose name the publisher believes will sell the book;
- those where the "author" is under no illusions about the saleability of his or her life story but wants to leave an account for his or her family; *and*
- those "vanity" projects where the "author" hopes or even believes that, once written, her or his life story will be attractive enough to a publisher for the publisher to pay the "author" and writer for it.

That last category is one I find hateful; I've been offered one or two and always refused them. I do, however, take on projects in the second category; for most new and unknown ghostwriters, they will be the only ones available.

If you decide to ghostwrite (and the money can be good, and sometimes very good indeed, and this is – after all – a book about making money as a freelance writer) there are a couple of things you need to be aware of. One is that the "author" won't understand why you take so long to deliver her or his book. She or he has done the hard work by telling you the story – all you have to do is to type it. If you're lucky in your "author", it may feel like that but in the huge majority of cases you'll find that you struggle to get enough usable words out of the subject to complete your contract.

However much you are paid, by the time you get to the end, you will know that you earned every penny.

And the second thing you need to know is that the "author" will almost always believe that they really are exactly that – that they wrote the book; if it attracts good reviews, they are the ones who earned them. When someone praised Ronald Reagan for his autobiography, he said, "I hear it's a terrific book. One of these days I'm going to read it myself." But Reagan was a man of rare self-awareness.

The acknowledged star among British ghostwriters today is Andrew Crofts who has written more than sixty books that between them have sold more than ten million copies. A man with a record like that deserves to be listened to and Crofts says that the most important quality in a ghostwriter is a complete lack of ego. If you want to ghostwrite, take a good honest look at yourself. Are you willing to be that self-effacing? He also says that it's necessary to be prepared to suspend moral judgement. If your subject has done something you don't approve of, you must not only ignore the fact – you must be ready to defend the subject against all comers.

And think of what you are writing as social history and not fiction (though, with some subjects, fiction is exactly what it will be).

When I think about Crofts's definition of a ghostwriter as someone with a complete lack of ego, I think, "I've never met one of those." I'd almost be prepared to say that the definition of a writer will almost always include the words "someone with an ego". The best I can do is to commit to suppressing my ego when writing autobiography. That will probably also be the best you can do.

At least one of the companies that publishes autobiographies for people to leave to their families and friends splits the duties of interviewer and writer, so you end up listening to, transcribing and then creating a draft of the book from an MP3 file created by someone else. Don't assume this will be easy. When I've interviewed someone with a view to transcribing the interview later, I take as much care as I can to produce a recording that will be clear, well-balanced (I mean in sound quality, not necessarily in the things people say), and free of extraneous noise. In my experience, most interviewers employed for this purpose either know they are not going to have to transcribe it later or don't even think about it.

I've had tapes where the person being interviewed had wandered off into the next room to make coffee or look for photographs but was still talking. The recording machine had stayed where it was. To hear the words, I had to crank up the volume as high as it would go – and that became painful when the interviewer, without warning, suddenly began to drum her fingers on the table or actually knocked over the microphone.

I've also had tapes where the interviewer apparently imagined that the book was going to be about her and not about the "author". I'd find myself thinking "Never mind what you learned at school or where you lived when you were five; I need to know about the author." That doesn't change the fact that you have to take what you've been given and turn it into a chapter of a book.

By the way, if you find yourself going out to interview someone, whether for autobiographies or for some other purpose, don't skimp on the recording equipment. You will regret it when it comes to transcribing. The gear I recommend is the Olympus LS-10, and I would pair it with the Olympus ME52W external microphone. They are professional standard and they'll give you professional results.

Copywriting and other sales material

By "sales material" I mean any kind of written material intended to sell a product.

I've placed my profile on a number of websites that can lead to business. On one of them, I wrote this:

> Copywriting is selling. That's what it is. If you're using copy that doesn't sell your products or services – Why? What is the point? And if copywriting is selling, the copywriter you need is someone who:
> - writes like an angel;
> - understands the impact of SEO and how to use it; and
> - can show you an illustrious career as a salesperson.
>
> That someone is me! Give me your hand and I'll lead you through the sometimes tricky byways of the English language. Where are we going? To business success, of course. What other goal is there?

I was a salesman for years and I have an instinctive feel for what makes people buy things as well as for what stops them doing so. I find that a great help when I'm copywriting. It isn't essential, however. Some very good writers indeed (Fay Weldon and Julian Barnes, to mention only two of a large number) have been copywriters with advertising agencies and they did not have my sort of sales background behind them. If you want to write copy (and you should, because it can be among the better paying freelance jobs) and you don't have a background in sales, study as many adverts as you can. Pick out the ones that make you think, "I might buy that". What is it about the way it's written and/or the way it's presented that attract you? Try to write in the same sort of way.

That expression "Copywriting," by the way, arouses all sorts of responses among those who've been around for some years. Copywriting is used to describe a wide range of material now and there's no shortage of people who will say, "That's not copywriting." Okay. I don't think arguing the point will get either of us anywhere. The technology has changed and the words are changing with it.

Press Releases

Press releases can be a good source of income because:

a) huge numbers of them are sent; *and*
b) most of those are not very good at all, which means that if you can show the ability to write a press release that captures a journalist's attention and gets its story into print, you'll be in demand.

Your press release will be sent by email. Journalists receive large numbers of emails every day and, as I said when talking about selling freelance work to newspapers, they don't have time to spare. You need to catch their attention with the subject of the email because if you don't they won't even open it. If they do open it you are still facing a very short attention span and the first line has to hit hard enough that they want to read the rest. Picture the journalist's default attitude as "I don't want to read this" and understand that you have to change that and you have almost no time to do it in.

Don't be tricksy. Write the subject header as though you were composing a headline and make sure it's easily understandable. Then, even though your opening paragraph must be as short as you can possibly make it, try to answer as many as you can of the journalist's time-honoured "Who, What, Where, When, Why" in your top line. (The "top line" is the most important part of your story and you'd better get it right at the beginning of the press release or the chances are it will never be seen).

The best way to learn how to write press releases is to read a bunch of newspaper stories – ideally, taken from the newspaper your client would really most like the story to appear in.

The advice normally given is that, if you printed it, a press release would fit on a single A4 page. Think 300 to 400 words. You can then add background information (but keep it short) on the company you're writing about (though they may well have this available as boilerplate) and – and this is essential – give the name, phone number and email address of the person the newspaper should contact if they want more

It's easier to get a press release for local news into a local newspaper for obvious reasons and a press release, however tedious, that tells people about next week's Women's Institute meeting in the village hall will always make it into print but if either your client's story or their ambitions run higher than that the most challenging part of your task may be finding an answer to the question: "Why should anyone care?" Write a few press releases about a metal-basher's latest sale to the Isle of Man and you'll find yourself asking: "Why indeed?" But it can be good money if you learn to do it right.

Stuff I don't do (1): Rewriting

Chapter 4 talks about where to find work as a freelance writer. You'll see reference there to agencies like Upwork and there's no question that Upwork can be a good source of business – I only signed up in November 2015 but now I find about 40% of my work there – but there are offers of types of work that I simply ignore. One of these is rewriting. It's presented in quite a straightforward way, and what it asks you to do is to take a piece of work that someone else has done and rewrite it in such a way as to foil Copyscape (see Chapter 2). In other words, you're expected to steal another writer's work. I won't do it; only you know whether you would be happy with the idea.

Stuff I don't do (2): CVs

Also on Upwork, and a number of other sites, you'll find agencies that write people's CVs (resumes if you're American). I don't have the same moral objections to this as I do to rewriting but it's badly paid and I find even thinking about it so boring that I can't imagine actually wanting to do it. It's there if you want it.

Stuff I don't do (3): Academic Writing

Academic Writing is how it's described by the agencies that offer it as work (though they may also say "Essay Writer"). Those agencies bring together students who need to submit an essay for a degree or other academic course and writers prepared to write it for them.

Look, it's up to you. You won't be paid very well and your work will be checked in Copyscape – at least, I hope for the sake of the student it will be checked – so you can't just plagiarise something you find online. I question the ethics of writing somebody else's essay, but you'll have to decide. If you do go for this, you'll be asked to show that you understand the major systems of citation.

Stuff I don't do (4): Social media

Of course, I do write social media because that's what blog posts are. I've also done the occasional Facebook post and most of my news items end up on Facebook and being tweeted and I'm usually at least one of the people who tweet them. The social media I don't do is:
- multiple tweets on the same subject
- multiple Facebook posts on the same subject

I don't do those things because the request is usually for ten, twenty, thirty or even more tweets or Facebook posts all fundamentally about the same thing and they bore me so much that before I get to the end I'm almost in tears. So I don't do them. I have enough work to choose and I choose not to do these things. If you are offered some when you first start out and feel you have no choice but to take them on, be aware that Copyscape will be used to compare them with each other and with other content on the Web, so you really will have to make sure that they are all completely different from each other.

Stuff I don't do (5): Product Reviews

Like for so much in this book, I find myself saying in relation to product reviews, "This is up to you." And although I've never done a product review, it isn't true that I wouldn't. For a product that I used regularly and liked, I wouldn't see a difficulty. What happens, though, is that people who are selling items know that they will do a lot better if the product has numerous positive reviews (testimonials is the word mostly used in the US although that word in the UK is generally restricted to something about a person) and so they pay people to write them. Bobby Fischer was chess champion of the world at one time and a man many would regard as "differently sane" but when he was asked to endorse some product or other for money at a time when he was close to penniless he said, "I don't use the stuff" and that was the end of that. I feel the same way. I don't know whether my moral objections to writing glowing reviews about something I don't use (or even something I have used and didn't think much of) make sense to everybody which is why I say, "This is up to you."

If you do decide to do product reviews, you may find that the person asking you to do them promises repeat business but that's unlikely to happen because they have realised that review sites notice when multiple reviews for one company's products are being written by the same person and they tend to delete them.

Chapter 4

How to find freelance work and how to win it

It's easy enough to get content mill work (see Chapter 1); just register with Copify and Upwork and respond to the ads people place there quoting a very low price for your work. You'll be competing with a lot of other low price bidders but apply for enough gigs and someone will take you on. There you are; you're writing five hundred words and you're going to earn five pounds for it. You're a freelance writer! Success!

But if that is success to you, then you're not really the sort of person this book was written for. If the occasional Copify gig or Upwork "Beginner's" job meets your aspirations, you didn't even need to read this far. My target audience is people who want to make enough money out of freelancing to pay all their bills without needing a day job.

Present a professional appearance

I don't mean you have to power dress before you sit at the PC; I'm writing this in an old pair of jeans, a *The Dude Prevails* T-shirt and no socks and I don't believe I shaved this morning. (I've just felt my chin and I can now confirm that I didn't shave this morning. Maybe tomorrow.) What I'm talking about when I say "professional appearance" is how you appear to the people you want to work for.

Logo

You need a logo. If you wonder why, click on this link: http://tabithanaylor.com/logo-design/. That explains the benefit of the logo as well as anything I've ever seen.

Your logo will go on various things that we'll talk about in a moment and it doesn't need to cost the earth but you should have one. You can see mine on my website; it isn't complicated but it says what I do and who I am. I use it a lot:

- on letterheads, invoices and quotations (see below)
- on my business card (see below)
- on the cover page of every portfolio I send out
- on my web pages and blog posts
- on my reports showing how I've analysed a job I've been asked to do and what I recommend

Business Cards

You need these, too. Once again, nothing complicated; mine says John Lynch, Freelance Writer on the front and on the back it has my logo, my name and what I do (again), and my mobile phone number, email address and the URL of my website. The only reason it doesn't also show my Skype address is that that would have made the card too "busy".

What I haven't included on the business card is as important as what I have. I don't show my home address or my home phone number. Those would be easy enough for anyone to find out but I don't normally want to be called there; if I do want somebody to call me at home, I'll write that number on the card but that rarely happens. As for the address, the fact that I live in what a lot of people would consider the back of beyond could be an advantage but it could also be a problem because some people will assume that you can't live where I do and still work successfully for large companies in urban centres.

That's actually nonsense and I can be in Manchester in an hour, in Birmingham in ninety minutes and in London inside three hours, but people have their prejudices.

I also selected the web page address and the email address with care. I have several email addresses and this happens to be the shortest so it fits best on the card, while the URL is for the specific page on a larger website and is the gateway to my work as a writer for hire.

Carry your business cards with you wherever you go. You never know who you are going to run into or get into conversation with and you'll look so much more professional if you can hand over a card rather than scribbling something on a piece you've torn off a newspaper. But if you do give someone a business card because the conversation suggested there might be work in it for you, do your very best to get theirs, too, so that when you get home you can send them a reminder email and a portfolio.

Letterheads

I have more than one of these; the one I use for freelance work has my logo on the left and, on the right, my name, Skype address, mobile telephone number, email address and the URL of my website.

As I said, I have more than one letterhead; the main difference is that the other has my physical address on it. I use that one as a packing list and dispatch advice when I'm sending something by courier or through the mail so that people will know exactly where it came from if it needs to be returned. If you're sending something in physical form to a company of any size, always include a packing list and dispatch advice and show their order number or other reference. Otherwise, you may get into an "it never arrived" argument later because it was delivered to Goods Inwards and the person there had no way to relate it to an order. (You think it's enough that you put on the label the name of the person who asked you to send it? Dream on).

You also need to use the letterhead for invoices. People you send an invoice to need your physical address in case they pay you by cheque but don't forget to include your bank details (sort code, account number and account name) so that they can pay direct by bank transfer. You'll usually get your money faster that way. But for heaven's sake double check the sort code and account number. If money meant for you goes to someone else because you gave the wrong details, it will be your fault and your loss.

Portfolios

The portfolio is very important. And for "portfolio" read "portfolios" because it's a serious mistake to send the same one with every request for work or job application. The portfolio needs to be tailored to:
- the people you're sending it to and the sort of business they're in
- the kind of work you are putting yourself forward for
- the style, tone and mood of the piece(s) you are proposing to write

Of course, when you're a beginner it's more difficult to put a portfolio together, either because you just haven't got enough to show or because you signed a nondisclosure agreement with your client. Concentrate on making copies and otherwise collecting every single thing you write. There's a folder on my hard disk called *Samples for Writing Portfolio* and, at first, everything went into it. When I had collected more than five hundred items there I became selective about what I added but I still put another three or four items in during an average week. I can imagine nothing more frustrating than knowing that, somewhere, you've written just the thing to show this client and you simply can't lay your hands on it.

Bear in mind, however, that just because you wrote something doesn't mean you have a right to reproduce it. You wrote it for a fee, you were paid, and at the moment when you were paid the copyright passed to the client. It isn't yours and you can't reproduce it in a portfolio without the client's consent. So ask. (Explain what you want to use it for, of course). Some clients will give you approval and some won't. Marketing companies that you write for who don't give you a byline are the least likely to agree because they may well see a benefit in allowing the client to believe that they write everything themselves. It's still worth asking, but don't be surprised if you're turned down.

(Actually, that isn't the story on copyright at all, but it's how it works. See Chapter 5 for more on this).

Social media

You certainly need a blog; I believe you also need a website. You almost certainly also need a presence on Facebook and that should be a professional page – keep it separate from where you post pictures of your father as a little boy or when you've drunk well but unwisely.

There used to be a saying that it was always the cobbler's children who had no shoes. The freelance writer's version of that is that they spend so much time writing posts for other people's blogs that they never have time to keep their own up-to-date. Try. And remember that the posts on your own blog and the pages on your own website need to be as good as the very best that you do because they are your shop front and it's on them that you will be judged. When someone follows a tweet or a Facebook page or a search engine link to the page where you sing your praises as a content writer, they will lose interest in you totally if they don't see a very model of the content writer's art.

Contracts

Your contract as a freelance writer won't always be drawn up by you, but you do need to have one. I've put the one I use as Appendix 1, and I find I use it in about 20% of the jobs I do. It's a good idea to keep contracts as short as possible, but there are some things that need to be covered:

- A Project Summary that simply says that you (the writer) have agreed with the client (the client) to carry out a job of work for a named sum of money
- Confirmation that the client has the power to enter into this contract with you on behalf of the client's organisation and will:
  * provide the necessary information on time
  * review the writer's work and provide feedback within the timescale set out in the contract
  * pay on time in accordance with the contract
- Confirmation that the writer has the ability to do the job, will carry it out professionally and will respect the confidentiality of the client's information
- A description of the assignment in sufficient detail to leave no room for argument on either side as to whether it has been properly completed, together with the client's right to changes and revisions

- Confirmation that copyright remains with the writer until payment in full has been received, at which point it passes to the client
- Deadlines
- Payment amounts and terms
- When and on what terms the contract can be cancelled

How do you fix your prices?

The range of charges by freelance writers is enormous. What I'm going to describe is how I decide what to charge; other people do things differently and you may well be one of them.

The vital thing for me is that I use voice recognition software. If I didn't, I couldn't operate as a freelancer. It would be a hobby that brought in a little pocket money instead of a serious occupation. That's because I simply could not produce with a keyboard anything like the number of words I do when I speak into a microphone.

At the centre of my calculations is the fact that I know, after more freelance gigs than I can count, that it takes me 50 minutes to produce a thousand words. By "produce" I mean research, dictate, edit, proofread and polish. A thousand words in 50 minutes means 1200 words per hour.

Knowing that allows me to convert cents per word into dollars per hour and dollars per hour into cents per word. Like this:

Method of Payment			
Cents Per Word		*Dollars Per Hour*	
¢ per word	= $s per hour	$s per hour	¢ per word
1¢	$12	$10	0.83¢
2¢	$24	$20	1.66¢
5¢	$60	$40	4¢ (approximate)
10¢	$120	$50	8¢ (approximate)

The reason that matters (apart from keeping track and comparing deals) is that some clients want to pay you by the hour and some by the word. From the client's point of view, neither of those methods is perfect. If they pay you by the word, how do they know you won't pad the piece out to make more money? And if by the hour, how do they know you've actually put in that number of hours?

I only have one client for whom I work on a "per hour" basis. Most of the others pay me a rate per word, but with two I have an agreement that I will write articles that conform to an approximate word rate (it may be five hundred words, in which case the piece I submit could be anywhere between four hundred and six hundred words) and I will be paid the same agreed amount whatever the actual length submitted.

I'm not going to work for $12 an hour and I'm not going to work for $24 an hour. That means I'm not going to work for one cent a word or two cents a word. You'll find when you launch yourself into the freelance marketplace that that means I rule out 75% of the work on offer – the content mill work. If you are the kind of writer this book is aimed at, you won't accept those figures either. (Believe me, they'll be offered to you.) As I've said before, the highest rate per word I currently get is six British pence which at the current rate of exchange equates to nearly nine US cents. That is high; I charge most of my work at either four cents or five cents a word, though I'm not now taking on anyone who won't pay a minimum of five pence or six cents. I've accepted less in the past when I really wanted the gig and I keep one client on who doesn't really pay me enough because I love the range of work she has, I like the fact that I get to brainstorm the subjects for a number of her clients so I end up writing what I want to write and, in any case, when she pays me each week she always adds a bonus. Anyone approaching me now though would find that six cents a word or sixty dollars an hour is the absolute minimum I'll accept.

What should you charge? Well, I hope what I've said so far tells you what a personal business it is but I recommend that you fix on an hourly rate that will allow you self-respect as well as giving you a worthwhile income. What I'm about to say assumes that English is your first language and you write it well. If those things are both correct, then I recommend that, in bidding for your first jobs, you don't go below a minimum of $20 an hour and that at an early stage (that is, as soon as you have two or three decent jobs to your credit) you raise that to $30 and then to $40.

More about Voice Recognition Software

I said earlier that, if I were not using voice recognition software (in my case, Dragon Professional), I would not be able to make the money I do as a freelancer. This is not because dictating is faster than typing, but because I am much more comfortable dictating than typing.

People who see me type often comment that I'm fast for someone who taught himself to type and was never trained. In fact, I've just done an online typing speed test and established that my typing speed is 35 words per minute. Trained typists doing the same test achieve scores of 65 words per minute or more, but even at 35 I would finish one thousand words in less than half an hour leaving time to edit, polish and proof read and still stay within my dictating speed of one thousand words in fifty minutes.

So it isn't speed that prevents me from being able to produce as many words by typing as I do by dictating. It's simply that I find dictating so much easier – so much more *me* – than typing. I couldn't keep going on the keyboard anything like as long as I can when speaking into the microphone.

And a wireless microphone makes it even easier, because the writer doesn't need to be sitting down all the time – you can get up, walk around, look out of the window, even walk into the next room and still keep writing.

How these things work for you may be different from how they work for me. What I will say is:

- unless you are absolutely comfortable and at home with the keyboard, give voice recognition software a try; *and*
- my 35 words per minute is slow by the standards of professional typists, but not when compared with most self-taught typists. If you are someone who types slowly with two fingers, always looking for the next key, then I really do suggest that, unless you start dictating, making decent money from freelance writing is almost certainly not for you.

Selling yourself

I originally put this section a little later in this chapter, but I think the things it says need to be heard as part of the pricing discussion.

Something that all successful salespeople have learned is: when to leave the negotiating table. There will be times as a freelance writer when you need to do that; to say, 'Thank you but I think it's clear we're not going to come to an agreement that suits both of us. Let's leave it there.' Say it politely, however irritated you may be, because:

a) you never know when you might want to speak to this person again, however much right now you may be thinking you won't; *and*
b) people can be malicious. It's amazing how many get pleasure from bad-mouthing someone who never did them any harm. Don't make an enemy you don't need.

I'll move away from writing to give an illustration of the kind of thing I mean (and I'm going to do that again in a moment, because selling your services as a freelance writer is no different from selling anything else).

I spent several years selling in the Middle East and I discovered something that happens a lot in – in particular – the United Arab Emirates (UAE). If you let it, the cheapest product sets the market price, even when the market knows the cheapest product is rubbish. I would visit someone who had a problem with the product he was buying (usually from China). It was cheap (let's say, twelve dirhams a piece: dirhams are the basic monetary unit of the UAE) but it broke early and even when it didn't break it stopped performing in a matter of months. They knew they should really be buying half a million or so a year but in fact they were buying double that number to make up for breakages and even that wasn't really enough.

So I'd show them something made in the UK that did the job perfectly, didn't break and lasted for three years. 'That's it!' they'd say. 'That's what we want!'

I'd tell them that was wonderful and our price was only fifteen dirhams.

'Oh, no,' would be the answer. 'The market price is only twelve. You have to meet the market price.'

In the early days, I'd enter into a discussion about how something that lasted three years instead of three months and only cost 25% more was actually a pearl beyond price (they like their pearls in the Middle East) and it would still be a bargain if we doubled the price. After a while, I stopped doing that; I learnt to shrug and say, 'The price is fifteen dirhams. You want it?' If they said yes I took the order; if they argued I learnt to say, 'I'm sorry, we're not going to agree. I'll stop taking up your time.'

And that's what you have to do. Set your price and don't budge. Say someone asks you to quote for a copywriting job that you reckon will take ten hours to do properly, and right now you're quoting $40 per hour. Quote $400. If they don't want to pay that but they do want to negotiate, your response depends on how much work you currently have and how much you want this gig. In my early days as a freelancer, I'd have joined in the negotiation. I don't now.

Which brings me to the second example extracted from my time selling in the Middle East. I got a call from a contractor who had messed up a very high profile project costing a huge amount of money. He was in serious trouble. I went to look at it and the problem (the mistake, because that's what it was) was obvious, and not big at all. (If you'd like to know what the problem was, I wrote a short story about it and you can find the story on my fiction blog here: http://tinyurl.com/n24rfob). I knew how to fix it and I told him so. I also knew that no one else in the country had the equipment needed to put the mess right. He asked me how much we'd charge.

Now, if he'd done the job right in the first place it would probably have cost about $10,000. Peanuts in relation to the total value of the job. Fixing it in place would be more expensive than that; to make a decent margin, I'd have to charge $18,000. What

I quoted was $80,000. I've no doubt he knew he was being gouged but he accepted the quote without question. He knew how limited his choices were.

The lesson? You have to stop thinking about the cost to you of doing a job and start asking yourself: "How much is it worth to the customer?" Here's something to print and stick on your wall:

The Key Question Is Not:

How Much Will It Cost Me?

But:

What Is It Worth To The Customer?

There will be times when the value to the customer of having the job done right isn't enough for the customer to be prepared to pay what it's worth to you to do it. Accept that and walk away. There will be other times, though, when the customer really knows the cost of not getting a good job done. Those are your times. But only if you charge enough.

And, of course, charging enough will be easier when you've already got some good work in your portfolio.

So where does the work come from?

Okay, enough about pricing and professional presentation; someone has the jobs you need. Who is it? Where are they? How do you get at them?

Finding Prospects

Every salesperson who ever lived has gone out looking for business. Begin by thinking about who your targets should be, and how you're going to approach them. In Chapter 2 I asked you to go through an exercise to work out a list of subjects that would tell you what you have that people might want to buy. Now you need to start offering your services. Initially (and this is apart from putting yourself on some registers, which I'll talk about in a moment) you should probably be making a list of possible targets selected from among the following:

- newspaper and magazine editors
- marketing companies and agencies
- individual companies with which you see a fit

Let's look at each of those in turn.

Newspaper and magazine editors
The magazines you list should be self-selecting. You know what your interests are and in what areas you are particularly knowledgeable; it's unlikely that there won't be magazines both in print and online that cater to those interests and areas. Begin by writing down the name of every one of them you can think of and then do an online search for more. Now you need to know who to approach because an email to info@blogsmail.com is probably not going to get you very far. Salespeople know that it's always best to target someone by name and I'm sorry to keep banging on about this but for this purpose you are a salesperson. One way of getting a name that works surprisingly often is to telephone the magazine's head office and ask the person who answers the phone. Don't try thinking up some clever and devious way of extracting a name because people know what you're doing and they don't like it. You might say, 'I wonder if you'd mind giving me the name of the editor?' Or, if there's one particular area of the magazine's coverage that interests you, ask for the person responsible for it. 'Could you help me, please? I'd like the name of the person responsible for reviews of SLR cameras.'

You'll get the name far more often than you might think, but confirm the spelling – always – and do that even when you think it's obvious. I've never come across more than one way of spelling "Henderson" but, even so, I'd still say, 'Thank you so much. Can I just confirm – that's H – E – N – D – E – R – S – O – N, yes?' And while you're doing it, please remember that the letter H is pronounced "aitch" and not "haitch". Haitch is one of the commonest solecisms practised in the British Isles and, while it may sound perfectly alright to some people, there will be others who will think, "You're an ignorant, ill-educated nowt and nowt is what I intend to have to do with you." I can tell you there are people who respond to that mispronunciation in that way, because I'm one of them. And if you think I'm a pedant, or simply wrong, look up "aitch" in the dictionary. Now look up "haitch." Convinced?

What you hope to sell to a magazine or a trade paper is an article on any subject that will interest their readership. The approach with newspapers is different because newspapers don't have one single area of interest to cover. What you need to decide is:

- will you approach national newspapers? Regional newspapers? Local newspapers? Or all three?
- what sort of work do you hope to get out of them? Opinion pieces? Local news items? Restaurant reviews? I could go on here…this list could probably contain more than 50 possible areas of interest and what you need to decide is what sort of approach is most likely to get a favourable response given

what you know, what the newspaper already has staff to cover and what is arousing interest right now.

Implicit in that last bullet point is that you don't approach a newspaper (or a magazine, for that matter) without doing some research first, and that means reading them often enough to get a feel for areas in which they are strong and those in which they are weaker. Look for names (and this is even more productive than telephoning because the editor's name will frequently be given in a newspaper or magazine and the people covering particular areas – for example, the business editor – will often also be named). What you'd like to find is that something about which you can write that doesn't have a regular writer's byline, because that suggests that there is no staff writer for that subject.

All right, you've done your research, you know who you're going to write to and what you'd like to interest them in buying. How do you compose your approach: letter or email? This is known as "the pitch" and I developed early on a motto that I still swear by. Print it and stick it on the wall near your computer where you can see it every morning:

> *A PITCH A DAY*
> *KEEPS THE BAILIFF*
> *AWAY*

Some things you probably need to know about editors:
- money is desperately tight. Forget those stories you grew up with about millionaire newspaper owners throwing vast amounts of money at writers. Today's editors don't have much to spend on their permanent staff, let alone on freelancers. And the huge sums newspapers pay to big-name columnists aren't an editorial cost at all – they come out of the marketing budget. Those names sell papers. Yours doesn't, and you won't be in that pay league.
- time is as short as money is and every editor receives far more pitches than she or he can ever use. The most assiduous pitcher will be lucky to get one assignment for every ten pitches. So either give up now or keep pitching. And bear that shortage of time in mind when not only do you not receive a rejection – you don't even get a reply. The best salesperson in the world (and who better than me to tell you this?) hears "No" far more often than "Yes" but the fact is that you will frequently hear nothing at all. If you pitched an

idea that you think still has currency and you haven't had a reply within 24 hours, pitch it to someone else. Although, really, you shouldn't have allowed it to reach that point. If as I recommend (see below) you made your initial approach by email, follow it up after about not more than three hours by email. Ask if the editor got it. At the very least that may get the editor to read the pitch and give you an answer

- the most important people in an editor's world are the advertisers. It's likely that some people probably still do go into journalism to wield "the simple sword of truth and the trusty shield of British fair play", but they soon get that knocked out of them by commercial reality. And let's never forget where those words came from (Jonathan Aitken) or what happened to him (he went to jail). My local newspaper spent months covering the story of a poor defenceless and friendless young woman who – innocently and inadvertently – knocked down a listed building of real merit and built in its place a modern home. The council obtained a court order instructing her to knock the new house down. The paper dwelt at some length on the iniquity of this action. And not once, in all the months the story dragged on, did the paper ever mention that the poor young woman was actually a daughter of the biggest and richest contracting firm for miles around or that the family, through its many interests, bought more than 60% of the paper's total advertising budget. If you write a story that in any way attacks or threatens the interests of a major advertiser, you won't sell it. So don't waste your time. That includes restaurant reviews. You may have irrefutable evidence that diners in a local eatery risk salmonella, lockjaw and an early death but don't try to interest the local paper. They'll be happy enough to run the story after the public health people close the place down (a closed restaurant buys no advertising) but if they run any reviews before that happens, the reviews will be full of praise for the quality of the food

The best approach to an editor is by email. Keep it short. Make sure the subject says what you are proposing to write about. Then in the body of the email say what it is you'd like to write about and give at least one reason why the editor should be interested. Then say who you are, who you've written for in the past and (if you can) provide two or three links to published pieces of yours. Attach a portfolio which should be both short and relevant. If you can't give links and you can't attach a portfolio, then you'll have to write the piece on spec and attach that.

Bear in mind when dealing with both magazines and newspapers that their deadlines are a lot further ahead than you may imagine. A newspaper will make room for an earth-shattering piece of news up to the last moment, but how many of those are there in the average year? Three? Most of tomorrow's paper (if it's a daily) will have been settled well before lunch today and if it's a weekly you have to sell your piece a lot earlier than that. As for magazines, they may already know most of what they are going to print six months from now.

Marketing Agencies

I write copy for two marketing agencies in the UK and one in the US. Something I'm very particular about is not telling any of the three who the other two are and not letting any of them see what I write for the others. It's possible that they would like to see what I do for the others but none of them would like to think that the others see what I do for them. Get a reputation for discretion.

And while we're on the subject, there will be times when a company for which you wrote something through an agency contacts you directly and asks you to write for them without involving the agency. What you do about that is up to you, but I always refuse. All I have to do is think "How would I feel if I brought business to someone who then cut me out?" I don't want to get a reputation among agencies for not being trustworthy.

What you want to know is how I got those agencies as clients. The answer is that I got each of them in a way that was different from how I got the other two. One came from Upwork, one from Indeed and one from a mailshot. I talk about Upwork and Indeed later in this chapter; right now I want to talk about that mailshot.

The first thing I did was to compile a list of every marketing agency that was an easy driving distance from where I live. That bit was easy enough; I did a search for "Marketing agencies in Shropshire" and then one for "Marketing agencies in Flintshire" and then one for "Marketing agencies in Cheshire." Then I added Birmingham and Manchester to the list. In each case, I clicked through to the agency's website. Then I read each website carefully to get contact names and the format of email addresses and to make notes on what differentiated them from others. (I said this was easy; I didn't say it was quickly done).

I then had a list of people I wanted to email; the next step was to prepare an email and a portfolio to go to each one of them. Of course I didn't write 62 different letters or put together 62 different portfolios (that's how many agencies were on the list: 62) but I did make changes in a number of the letters to use things I picked up on the websites that were different about specific agencies and in some cases I put an extra item or two into the portfolio because I thought it went with the work they did for the clients they had.

The reason I did that (and still do it, whether I'm approaching a marketing agency or someone else) is because I don't want to be kicked into the long grass. By far the most frequent reason for being turned down by a marketing agency is that they already have a writer or writers (quite possibly on the staff rather than freelance) and at the moment they receive your letter they don't need any more. The second reason, though, is because they see you as a generalist and when it comes to marketing most companies want someone they see as a specialist in their field. So, any time I have the chance to show that I understand and have already worked in that field, I take it. You should do the same.

I have, as I've said, one marketing agency that came from those sixty-two letters and for whom I work regularly but there are three others who have given me the occasional piece to write when their in-house writers were overloaded. Four results out of sixty-two is pretty good going, because the typical response rate to direct mail postcard marketing is 3.7% and for email marketing it's less than a 10th of 1%. This is an example of the sort of email I sent.

> Dear ....
>
> When I retired from my job in international sales, I planned to write full-time. I still do – I've published *The International Sales Handbook* and three novels – but writing is a solitary business and I'm a gregarious person. One of the reasons I continued to travel the world looking for new business was – I thought – because I enjoyed meeting new people and solving new challenges. I now know that that was only a partial explanation. It's not just enjoyment; I *need* the interplay with other people. And so, as well as continuing to write fiction, I have gone back to something I have done before: freelancing as a writer for hire.
>
> The attached portfolio will give you the flavour of what I write. You can find more samples of my work as a freelance writer here and an account of how I work here. I'm available for the shortest assignments and the longest

> – I've written single paragraph company profiles, four page product brochures, 50 page sales proposals and 50,000 word books. I'm looking for a freelance role and not a full time position; if you think I can fill a hole for you, please get in touch.
>
> (Oh – and the novels I retired to write? You'll find them <u>here</u>. And right now there's a 30% discount offer with free postage, so you can settle your Christmas gift needs without leaving home ☺)
>
> Best wishes

You might think there's nothing tailored there, but in fact I wrote that in that way because the agency I was addressing has clients who export and I wanted to get across the message that I understand their business and speak their language.

Before leaving this section, some more reasons why you may have trouble with marketing companies and can lose them as clients:

- they think you are too sure of your own opinions and don't listen to them
- they see that you don't pay enough attention to the brief and they regularly get back from you material that isn't close enough to what they asked for
- they don't feel that you research hard enough or widely enough to deliver what the client needed

Companies

I wrote (and still write) on spec to companies in the same way as I wrote to marketing agencies, but I gathered the company names and contact details in a different way. What I do in this case is to scan (online) the business pages of papers like *The Birmingham Post*, *The Manchester Evening News* and *The Shropshire Star* and what I'm looking for is stories about companies that are relatively small but have signed some major contract or are otherwise expanding. The newspaper item will almost always have names and job titles that I can use. Then I go to the company's website and look for contact details.

Sometimes the website will have a "News" section and when you go there you find the name of a marketing agency representing them. Is that agency on your list? If not, add it and consider whether you want to contact them using the piece of news that brought you to this website as a trigger. What you really want, though, is a site where the contact for news is given as the company's marketing manager or director. Chances are that person already has agencies that work for the company in specific areas and one of those may be a writer but if your pitch is good enough you may well be offered a test piece.

If there is no News section, get the contact details and write direct either to the head of marketing or, if you can't find one of those, to the most senior person whose details you have.

It's hard work

You will have gathered by now that prospecting for work is a matter of thought and concentrated effort and not something you can be casual about. You're competing with a lot of people and early success will depend on whether you work harder than they do. It does get easier in time and I'll say some more about that after I've talked about the other places to find work.

Upwork

I've been on Upwork a relatively short time because at first I ignored it and that was the wrong thing to do. If you're a freelancer you need to be on Upwork. It can be frustrating, but there is good business to be done there as well as bad.

Upwork came into being when two earlier operations, Elance and oDesk, merged. It's based in California and spreads its tentacles worldwide; it has millions of freelancers on its books (not all of them are writers; they have editors, proofreaders, graphics designers, programmers, software developers – you name it); some of them are very good indeed and many would need to work very hard to raise themselves to the level of "appalling." You're competing with the appalling ones as well as the good ones and they are prepared to work for close to nothing. Since "close to nothing" is what many of the people advertising jobs there want to pay, I assume that they find themselves a good fit with each other. You will meet freelancers who will tell you that Upwork is a waste of time and you can't make any money there but it isn't true. I make anywhere from $200 to $800 on Upwork every week (usually closer to $200 to $300, but I've had those $800 weeks) and at the moment Upwork gives me about 40 percent of my freelance earnings although that percentage is falling.

You'll find Upwork at Upwork.com and the first thing you have to do is register there. You won't be alone; when you go to their Messages page they like to give you little snippets of information and one will be to tell you how many new freelancers have joined in the past week. Don't let it get you down because if you are any good then most of them won't be competition for you.

When you register, give the amount that you are prepared to work for per hour. Work that comes through Upwork is either hourly paid or at a fixed rate. The hourly rate always strikes me as odd and I only have one customer for whom I work that way. "Odd" because until the client knows how many words you can write in an hour she or he has no idea what the work is going to cost. The one hourly-paying customer I do have didn't give me much work at first because they had other writers whose hourly rate was less than half of mine. That changed when they discovered that I worked more than twice as fast as the "cheaper" writers, so my finished articles actually cost less. I much prefer to work on a fixed rate and, if I were looking for someone to work for me, I would only be prepared to offer a fixed rate. For writing jobs, the fixed rate may occasionally mean, for example, "£50 for a blog post" but usually it will be a rate per word.

Membership on Upwork is free; they make their money by charging a commission on everything you earn. The rate changed after this book went to the typesetter; I blogged about the changes here: ~ http://tinyurl.com/gwr6olv.

I've heard people moaning about that commission, but I'm happy to pay because you are getting more than just a series of ads. Upwork makes sure you get paid. They take the money from the customer and hold it in escrow until you've done the job. There's more to it than that, which I'll say something about later in this section, but I've never failed to be paid for an Upwork job I've done, wherever in the world the customer happened to be, and that's worth paying for.

Upwork has a series of tests you can take and I suggest that you do because they are an indication to people who might hire you of the quality of work you're likely to be able to do. These are the tests I have done:

Tests

Name	Score (out of 5)		Time to Complete	Display on profile	
UK English Grammar Test (For Writing Professionals)	3.60	Top 10%	18 mins	Yes	No
UK English Proofreading Skills Test (Oxford Guide to Style)	3.25	Top 10%	21 mins	Yes	No
UK English Basic Skills Test	4.75	Top 10%	12 mins	Yes	No
Technical Writing Skills Certification	4.00	Top 10%	14 mins	Yes	No
Online Article Writing and Blogging Test (U.S. Version)	4.60	Top 10%	12 mins	Yes	No
Content Writing Skills Test	3.75	Top 10%	15 mins	Yes	No
English Spelling Test (UK Version)	4.60	Above Average	6 mins	Yes	No

I took that from my Upwork Profile; as you will see, the button on the right allows you to choose not to show it there and you would make that decision if you thought one or more of your results was not good enough to show people. That brings me to the subject of your Profile and you need to complete it. Click on all the skills you want to offer on Upwork and give an overview of your ability and interests. This is currently mine:

Overview

Copywriting is selling. That's what it is. If you're using copy that doesn't sell your products or services – why? What is the point? And if copywriting is selling, the copywriter you need is someone who:
    a. Writes like an angel;
    b. Understands the impact of SEO and how to use it; *and*
    c. Can show you an illustrious career as a salesperson.

> That someone is me! Give me your hand and I'll lead you through the sometimes tricky byways of the English language. Where are we going? To business success, of course. What other goal is there?
>
> My career as writer for hire dates back to 1989; in addition, I've worked in international sales on every continent except Antarctica. My books include *The International Sales Handbook* ISBN 978-1-910194-05-8 and *Managing The High Tech Salesforce* ISBN 978-1-850581-25-3 as well as three novels. I'm available for the shortest assignments and the longest – I've written single paragraph company profiles, four-page product brochures, 50 page sales proposals and 50,000 word books. I'm looking for freelance roles and not a full time position. If you think I can fill a hole for you, let's talk.

As you will notice, I'm not too shy to tell people how good I am. I blow my own trumpet in a very non-British way. And so must you, because most of the jobs offered on Upwork are not British. Most of the ones I've actually accepted are American, but you'll find an enormous range of countries represented.

Stepping out of Upwork for a moment to pursue that subject, at the same time as writing this book I'm making a new blog for myself. The front page contains this:

> I'm unashamedly at the top end when it comes to pricing; I know how good I am and I'm only interested in working with people who want real quality. There's a market for all those non-English-speaking non-writers who work for a cent a word but you won't find me there. If you know the best when you see it, fill out this form; I'll put you on the mailing list for my newsletter and, when you ask me to, I'll contact you to discuss your projects.

Blow your own trumpet. You can't rely on anyone else doing it for you.

Right. Back to Upwork. The next thing to attend to is your portfolio. Upload pieces that show the variety of the work that you do. A good range is more important than a large number. Then, under "Employment History," enter what you want to about your work history.

So now your Upwork account is set up. But how do you find the ads? How do you look for a job? Strangely enough, by clicking on the "Find Work" button at the top of the Upwork page, and then on "Find Jobs":

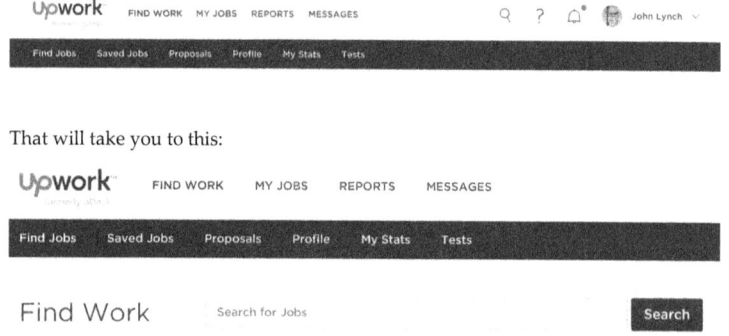

That will take you to this:

Once you've done this for the first time, you'll see your "Job Feed" below that box, but ignore it. Type "Writer" into the box that says "Search for Jobs". A multitude of jobs will be listed, but first turn your attention to the column on the left of the screen. For convenience, I've split it in two; the two columns I'm showing here actually appear one under the other:

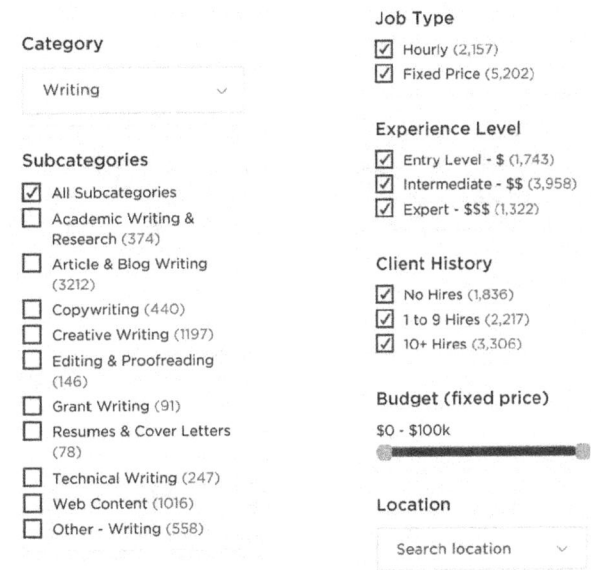

This gives you the opportunity to break down the huge number of jobs to a more manageable list. I've taken the first step already by selecting the category "Writing"; you may have assumed that since I asked for writing jobs, that's all that would be listed but you'll find when you do this searching yourself that all sorts of other categories are included. Once you get to writing, there's a whole host of subcategories which are listed on the left. If there are any that don't appeal to you (which in my case would include: the 374 academic writing and research jobs; the 146 editing and proofreading jobs; the 91 grant writing jobs; and the 78 resume cover letter jobs), then uncheck the "All Subcategories" box and instead check only the boxes for jobs you'd like to do.

Now decide what experience level you are interested in. I would immediately uncheck the "Entry Level" and "Intermediate" boxes because I'm not interested in low-paying jobs. There will still be plenty of low-paying jobs even at Expert level because the ability of advertisers to delude themselves into imagining that they can get first class writing for peanuts knows no bounds, but at least you will have eliminated most of those who know that what they are prepared to pay won't attract anyone of any ability. I say "most" because Upwork's searching isn't perfect and, even when you have indicated that you only want the Expert ads, you'll still find a number of Intermediate and some Beginner level jobs among those that are shown to you.

I've sometimes thought it would be a good idea to uncheck under "Client History" the "No Hires" box because doing that would reduce the number of scams, but I don't recommend doing so because I have seen good jobs advertised by people who were on Upwork for the first time. When you're starting out, you probably won't uncheck the "Hourly" job rate, but after you've been doing Upwork jobs for a while you probably will. It was actually while writing this chapter that I decided to offer my only client who pays by the hour the option to convert to a rate per word or to find another writer.

A lot of the advertisements you find will discourage you but there are jobs there that will provide a good writer with a good income. Here's an example, chosen at random:

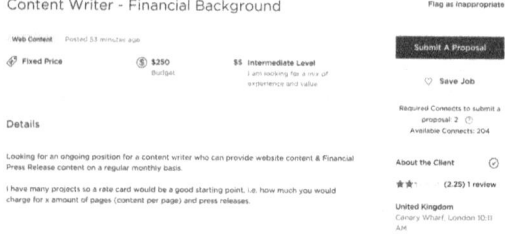

This is no use to me because I don't have the financial background, but someone could make use of it. They might want to check on the client first, because there is one freelancer review with only two stars – I personally would want to see what that reviewer said before going any further.

On the right, you'll see that you have the opportunity to save this job to come back to later or to submit a proposal. Under the "Submit a Proposal" button, you will see that it says you need two "Connects" to apply and that there are 204 "Connects" available. A number of Connects are allocated to you free of charge when you sign up with Upwork and they are renewed each month; if you need them, you can buy more by paying $10 each month. The 204 means that when I did that job search I had 204 unused Connects.

When you see an Upwork advertisement that you want to apply for, click on the "Submit a Proposal" button. You will be taken to a page that allows you to send the advertiser a covering letter and a portfolio up to a maximum two megabytes in size. Spend some time on composing that covering letter. Make it relevant to the ad – don't just use the same letter for every job you apply to. You're being assessed as a writer, for heaven's sake, and a writer who will be expected to produce relevant copy. If there are additional questions to be answered, they will turn up here. If the ad requires that you include a specific word or words in your cover letter (see below) then do so.

Upwork says that most clients hire within three days and that may be so, but I've known people take two or three weeks to invite someone for "interview." I've put that word in inverted commas because it isn't really an interview – you may be asked for more information or just to confirm what you're going to do. You will almost never hear from a client who doesn't want you, but Upwork will sometimes let you know that you've been rejected. And sometimes they won't. If you don't hear anything, assume you didn't get the job. If you want to, you can go back and look at the original advertisement (do this by clicking on the "Proposals" link at the top of the Upwork page) and see how many people they interviewed and whether or not they've made an offer.

Now I'm going to take a sample job advertisement on Upwork and work through it. I chose this entirely at random and I am not expressing a view, positive or negative, on the opportunity itself or the person advertising it. The purpose of what I'm doing here is to show how to read an ad. I'll work through the various parts to give you a clear understanding of what's happening.

Hire US, Canada Content Writer - $2/100 Words - Trial Job Needed

Flag as inappropriate Thanks for flagging!
Article & Blog Writing Posted 1 hour ago
Fixed Price
Budget **$5,000**

$$$
Expert Level
I am willing to pay higher rates for the most experienced freelancers

That's the opening section and it consists of:
- a header saying what is being looked for (a content writer from either the US or Canada)
    - what the pay will be (two cents a word)
    - a condition – the advertiser wants anyone who applies to do a trial job; it doesn't say here whether the trial will be paid for
- a place to click if you find the ad "inappropriate" (which usually means you suspect it of being a scam; I'll say more about that in a while)
- a summary of what is being asked for
- the fact that this is a fixed-price contract and not hourly paid
- an indication that the advertiser is ready to pay up to $5000
- three dollar signs indicating that the person they are looking for should be Expert Level, followed by the definition of "Expert Level" in Upwork terms (willing to pay higher rates for the most experienced freelancers). The other levels on Upwork are "Beginner" and "Intermediate".

Note that the header does not need to contain anything like the amount of information this one does, and most are far less forthcoming.

Details

Hire 2 Freelancers

We are looking for an experienced English writer to write articles for my niche sites. This is a long term job. The quality of writing should be outstanding. We will pay $2 for each 100 words (fixed)

Key requirements:

- Personal writer, not company or team. (If your work done well, I will have more jobs for you)
- Have experienced in the product review, call to action.
- Native in English, excellent grammar, no spelling errors.
- Article must be 100% fresh and pass Copyscape (I will provide subjects, guidelines)
- Deliver articles on time follow my requirements.
- We will have the ownership of the articles.
- Applicants must be "Khoi" at the beginning of your application subject. If not, i will ignore.

Please let me know if you have any questions.

----- NOT for anyone who do not interest in this requirements -----

Regards,

- **Other Skills: Article Writing Blog Writing Content Writing**

On the right-hand side of this advertisement it tells you that the advertiser is based in Vietnam, so there's no need to look down on the quality of the English. That's what he wants to pay a writer for. You will note that he wants the quality of writing to be "outstanding"; I personally think you have to be ready to pay more than two cents a word to get truly outstanding writing. I certainly wouldn't take this job on, and one of the reasons is that it doesn't pay enough. The other is that the job is to write product reviews and I said in Chapter 3 that I would only do that for a product I was particularly interested in and used. Nevertheless, this is a real ad and the purpose of going through it is not to say "I wouldn't do this" but to explain how job ads on Upwork work. The sixth bullet point says "We will have the ownership of the article" and my response to that would be: Of course you will – the moment you've paid. Copyright remains with the writer until the writer has been paid.

"Applicants must be 'Khoi' at the beginning" is a typo; for "be" read "write." A lot of advertisers do this; asking applicants to begin with a set word or phrase is a way of avoiding automated responses. I've no idea why this advertiser says the job is not for anyone who is not interested in it – I should have thought that was obvious.

You will be asked to answer the following questions when submitting a proposal:
Do you have experience in writing articles about product reviews?
Can you send me some product reviews which you wrote before? I want to have a reference.
Do you have any experience in writing articles about home improvement?

This is something you will see quite frequently in Upwork advertisements. The advertisers want some extra information about the applicant's experience in order to home in on those who most closely meet their requirements. This is also quite useful because it tells you what the job is, which is to write product reviews, and that the product area is to do with home improvements.

.Proposals (9)
See current bids for this job
Bid range - High $5,000.00 | Avg $1,185.89 | Low $1.00

Freelancer	Proposal date	Initiated by
Chimerenka Odimba	7 hours ago	Freelancer
Joshua M.	7 hours ago	Freelancer
John Paul Heje Nick	7 hours ago	Freelancer
Stewart Lacey J.	7 hours ago	Freelancer
Maureen K. Michael	7 hours ago	Freelancer
Boaz Tarun Kumar	7 hours ago	Freelancer
Ronald C.	7 hours ago	Freelancer
	8 hours ago	Freelancer
	8 hours ago	Freelancer

This section shows what proposals have so far been received. There are nine of them and the prices quoted range from a high of $5000 to a low of a dollar. Ignore the average figure because it's meaningless. There's a list of who the bidders are and clicking on the names will tell you more about them. If you're wondering why anyone would bid one dollar, I'm afraid I can't help you.

Client's Work History and Feedback (9)
Jobs in progress

Content Writer $1 / 100 Words - Need High Quality Content
Writer *Job in progress*
Freelancer Carlos Sabio
Feb 2016 - Present

Content Writer $1 / 100 Words - Need High Quality Content
Writer *Job in progress*
Freelancer Charline B.
Feb 2016 - Present

Need Article Writer (500-2000word) - This is a long term job
Job in progress
Freelancer Joemar S.

Nov 2015 - Present

Need Article Writer (500-2000word) - This is a long term job.
No feedback given
To Freelancer: Irene Frances Mae L. Cabrera No feedback given
Mar 2015 - Jul 2015
Fixed Price $2.30

Need Article Writer (500-2000word) - This is a long term job.
Nguyen is a great client. He pays on time. More
To Freelancer: Mary faith S. No feedback given
Mar 2015 - Jul 2015
Fixed Price $2.30

I need writer to help generate high-quality content(product reviews) for my niche sites.
I worked second time for Khoi and looking forward to a great long term working relation with the client. More
To Freelancer: Sneha Agrawal
Jul 2014 - Jul 2014
Fixed Price $11.70

I have a need for several excellent article writers to write articles (500-2000word).
Great Client. very Professional and I am awaiting more work from him. More
To Freelancer: Arunaday Basu
Jul 2014 - Jul 2014
Fixed Price $2.30

I need writer to help generate high-quality content(product reviews) for my niche sites.
The client is really appreciative and I am looking forward to work for a longer term with the client. More
To Freelancer: Sneha Agrawal
Jul 2014 - Jul 2014

Fixed Price $2.30

(1) more

Other open jobs by this client (3)

- Content Writer $1 / 100 Words - Need High Quality Content Writer - Fixed Price
- Content Writer $1.5 / 100 Words - Need High Quality Content Writer - Fixed Price
- Content Writer $1.5 / 100 Words - Need High Quality Content Writer - Trial Job Needed - Fixed Price

Now, this section is very useful because it tells you what jobs this advertiser has advertised in the past and what he or she paid for them. As you can see, it generally speaking wasn't very much, so – at least in the past – we have to assume that the client has accepted low bids. There is one final part of this advertisement that is worth looking at. This one:

>About the Client
>(4.97) 5 reviews
>Vietnam
>Can Tho 12:12 AM
>13 Jobs Posted
>39% Hire Rate, 4 Open Jobs
>$135 Total Spent
>9 Hires, 3 Active
>Member Since Jun 17, 2014

The first useful thing this tells us is that he's been an Upwork customer since June, 2014 which is 18 months before the current advertisement was placed, and that in that time he has posted 13 jobs and hired nine people. That means that he is a genuine Upwork client and not a scam artist and, as I said a few sentences ago, I'll be saying more about that in a moment. We also know that, for the nine completed jobs, he has paid a total of $135. You might want to bear that in mind if you're attracted by the budget figure of $5000. It's always worth looking at the information Upwork gives you and comparing what has happened in the past with what is being suggested for the future. I'm not suggesting in any way that this client is not a good one to do business with, though I personally don't do product reviews and, even if I did, I wouldn't work for that amount of money per word.

You may feel differently.

I've mentioned scams a couple of times. I don't apply for many jobs on Upwork, so it's interesting to me that given the very few number I do respond to, two of them have been scams. That's what that "Click if inappropriate" button is for – to report a suspicious advertisement. In my experience, Upwork is very quick to respond.

The first scam I encountered claimed to be posted by a young American woman who really does exist (though I very much doubt that she had anything to do with this; it looks like identity theft to me). It claimed to be posted from America and offered to pay four cents a word. It said "You should be available on Skype 24/7 with effective communication" and it gave a Skype address which, once again, appeared to be the Skype address of a young American woman. I applied (through Upwork, not on Skype), and was invited to interview though I didn't read anything flattering into that; the ad showed that everyone who applied was invited to interview.

The interviews were scheduled for the following Sunday and I imagine that Sunday was chosen because the perpetrators believed that Upwork supervisors would be less active on that day. At 7.31 in the morning UK time (which would be in the middle of the night anywhere in the US from where this message was supposed to be coming, but mid-morning in Eastern Europe which is where I believe it did originate) this Skype conversation took place by text messaging:

▇▇▇▇ Hello John. How are you??
John Lynch: Hi, Lisa. I'm fine, thanks. You? (And shouldn't you be asleep? :-))
▇▇▇▇: I am working, till late
John Lynch: Clearly :-)
▇▇▇▇: Yes now John we have a company
John Lynch: Aha?
▇▇▇▇ We pay per page (275 words)
John Lynch: Okay. How much per page?
▇▇▇▇: We pay from 13-18 per page
▇▇▇▇: Depending on quality
▇▇▇▇: We have unlimited work(as many pages as you want)
John Lynch: I have space (comfortable, that is -- without over stretching myself) for up to five pages a day.
▇▇▇▇: Okay
▇▇▇▇: We however, have a 32$ fee for our panel
John Lynch: You ask the writer to pay $32 for work?

███████: For commitment purposes, its refundable

John Lynch: Lisa, I'd need to see that there really was work there before I paid that. So I'll offer this: you give me some pages (at least $32 worth) and you can deduct the $32 from the first payment. That shows commitment. How does that sound?

███████: But Sir, that's our policy, we have many writers who paid that and are currently working and comfortable

John Lynch: I'm sorry, Lisa, we're not going to agree. Give me three pages and I'll do them free of charge, so there's your $32 plus change -- but I don't know any of these writers and I don't, with all respect, know you and I'm not handing over money in advance. That's MY policy :-)

███████: Okay John, then we will have to go for the next writer, thanks for your time and have a great time. Bye :)

John Lynch: So long.

███████: What?

███████: Long?

John Lynch: "Good Bye". So long, it's been good to know you -- it was a song before you were born.

███████: Ok

I passed this Skype transcript to Upwork with the comment that I very much doubted that it was legitimate and they replied very quickly (even though it was Sunday) that they agreed, the ad was a scam and it had been removed from the site.

My experience is typical, you're going to be on the receiving end of scams not infrequently when you look for jobs on Upwork. To their credit, Upwork sort them out very quickly when you press the "inappropriate" button. The best way to avoid them is to follow Upwork's own rules:
- communicate only through Upwork's in-house messaging service (which works very well and you can upload files)
- never pay the advertiser a penny. That's one of the conditions on which Upwork accepts their ad in the first place.

Upwork pays five days after the job has been approved by the customer. If it's an hourly paid job, the week closes on Sunday, the customer has till the end of the following week to raise any objections and you'll be paid the Wednesday after that. Otherwise, it's five days after approval, seven days a week. You can choose to be paid to your bank account or your PayPal account; I use PayPal because transfer is almost instantaneous whereas it can take days for the money to reach your UK bank account from America. They deduct a one dollar processing fee every time they pay you.

Copify

Copify is a content mill, pure and simple. It has been vilified by freelancers as one of the organisations through which freelancing has been devalued and the fees received by freelancers depressed. It's true that jobs advertised on Copify tend to be (a) mostly very short and (b) poorly paid – I've only once seen a job there at more than one penny a word. The UK address for Copify is http://uk.copify.com/; if you're outside the UK just miss out the "UK." Then click on the Menu item "WRITERS" and you will be taken to a screen where you can take a test to be admitted to Copify as a freelance writer. I have no idea whether anyone ever fails this test, although the site does make the claim "We have the biggest and best network of quality copywriters in the UK. They are all rigorously assessed, so we are confident that they will exceed your expectations." It goes on to say that only UK writers are used. Once you are registered, you will receive an email every day that looks like this one:

Browse all open orders

Blog [Health and Fitness, 350 words] Health and Fitness Blog 350 words   Pays **£3.50**

Blog [Internet, 350 words] Internet Blog 350 words   Pays **£3.50**

Blog [Legal, 350 words] Legal Blog 350 words   Please say that again **£3.50**

Blog [Technology, 350 words] Technology Blog 350 words   Pays **£3.50**

Blog [Technology, 350 words] Technology Blog 350 words   Pays **£3.50**

Blog [Other, 350 words] Other Blog 350 words   Pays **£3.50**

10 Scottish sayings that every Glasgweigian student must know Other Blog 400 words   Pays **£4.00**

great-deals-to-agadir Travel Web Page 400 words   Pays **£4.00**

Town Bathrooms - Showroom Bathroom Web Page 200 words   Pays **£2.00**

Blog [Building and Construction, 350 words] Building and Construction Blog 350 words   Pays **£3.50**

Mobile Roulette Casinos Web Page 2000 words   Pays **£20.00**

As you will see, they are all penny-a-word jobs. You can also log onto the Copify site and click on your dashboard for a list of all the jobs that are available. I clicked on the third one on the above email and this is what I got on my screen:

Blog [Marketing, 350 words]

#92946 Posted in Marketing 4 days, 23 hours ago

Status
OPEN

Order type
Blog

Words required
350

Deadline
Today, 17:00

Pays
£3.50

Please write a blog post about "Marketing".
This post will be published on the following blog: http://colourfulowl.com/blog
Review all existing posts on this site before deciding on a subject that has not yet been covered and for style and tone guidance.
Include one or more of the following keywords in your post where relevant: Inbound Marketing, Marketing Automation, Website Development, Website Design, Marketing Funnel, Marketing Strategy, Marketing Support, Marketing, Email Marketing, Leads, Marketing Manchester, Email Development, Social Media, Social Media Strategy, Social Media Marketing, Search Engine Optimisation, sharability, Colourful Owl,

Some topics we've already covered and want to avoid:
Optimising for shareability on social media
Binge content, micro moments and the reshaping sales funnel
Accept this order. Due Today, 17:00

I've actually missed out some of the text because it was about the intentions of the company placing the ad and dealt with matters extraneous to this book.

If the ad appeals, you click the button at the bottom and the job is yours. Finish it by the time indicated, send it (you'll find as a button for that, too) and you'll get paid.

Now, I don't have any views on Copify one way or the other but I didn't use it because I'm not prepared to work for a penny a word. For the purposes of this book, however, I felt I needed to put it to the test so I clicked on a 1600 word, £16 job that asked for four blog posts of about 400 words each. I did the job and I was paid on time; I also got a very nice message from the advertiser telling me I was an excellent writer and they looked forward to using me again. In fact, they won't use me again because – at the risk of boring you – I won't work for a penny a word but I have tested the system and it works just fine.

If I had clicked on all five jobs, I'd have ended up writing 2,550 words for £25.50. At the speed at which I write, proof read and edit, that would have taken me just over two hours so I'd have been working for £12 an hour. I'm not going to do that. You may feel the same. However (and let me tell you that an awful lot of the people you write for will intensely dislike a sentence that begins with "however"), it might be attractive to someone just starting out and needing to get a few jobs under their belt. There were actually a total of twelve jobs listed on that email, so clicking on all of them would have brought in about £60 and (provided that you got the agreement of the people you wrote for) you'd have something to put in your portfolio to help you start the upward climb.

Fiverr

Another content mill. I have to list Fiverr here for the sake of completeness, but I've never taken a Fiverr job and I can't tell you much about it. There's a UK site at https://uk.fiverr.com/ and the original American site at https://www.fiverr.com/. Go there, join and click on the "Start Selling" button.

The site gets its name from the fact that originally every job was done for $5 and that's still the basis (though it's £5 on the UK site). What you'll see is people asking for writing jobs to be done and you can quote for "extras" to get the price up, but my feeling about this site is that it's a place for cheap jobs done for cheap people. (You can judge what I think of it myself when I tell you that I've had two graphics jobs done there for five dollars each – but there we get to the heart of what I think of as "the Fiverr problem". To get a good book cover done by a professional will cost you anything between £300 and £500. I asked someone on the subcontinent, in return for five bucks, to design a cover for this book. What she sent me looked okay. It did the job. It had a nice picture on it. And that picture was the problem. I didn't believe she'd taken it herself and I wondered… I copied the pic and put it into Tin Eye (a useful site; you'll find it here: https://www.tineye.com/). Sure enough, someone else held the copyright to that image and, if I used it on my book, I have laid myself open to a hefty charge. That's not Fiverr's fault, of course, but you do need to be very careful about what you're "buying").

Anyway, once again, if what you want is to get started and build a portfolio, there may be worse ways of doing it than on Fiverr.

Advertisements

People advertise in the press and on online job sites for freelance writers. One of the biggest is Craig's List; I don't use it and if you Google it you'll find no shortage of comments about it. I do use Indeed (http://www.indeed.co.uk/). Go to that site and register. There's a place for you to upload your CV (resume if you're reading this in the States) and I suggest that what you actually upload should be a PDF file with a brief CV as the front page and four or five items from your portfolio behind it. When you decide to reply to an Indeed advertisement, you have the opportunity to upload a different CV which means that, if appropriate, you can change the items for a specific application.

Indeed emails advertisements to you every day. You'll find that more than half of them are for medical writers, so if you have expertise there you should find no shortage of work. I don't, but I've found two well-paying jobs on Indeed in the last month, so clearly it's a site that freelancers should be looking at.

There are other boards that advertise writers' jobs and, if you're short of work, it's a good idea to do a regular search on your search engine of choice for "freelance writer." All sorts of things will turn up, of course, and among the jobs you see listed will be some that were filled months ago, but you will find some current ones.

Other people will find them too, of course – lots of other people – so the way you word your application will be crucial. Here is one I used recently and it got me the job:

> Good morning
>
> My freelance writing career began in 1989. Apart from occasional *ad hoc* assignments, I currently have four regular clients:
> - an American marketing company for whom I write blog posts;
> - a British marketing company for whom I do the same;
> - a news site based in Portugal for which I write anything between two and five news items each day; *and*
> - a ghostwriting company.
>
> I attach a portfolio that covers quite a wide range; you can find more about my freelance work here: http://tinyurl.com/ngbjjmr. Ignore the "Terms of Business" page – that's only for one-off assignments that come to me through the blog. My rate for regular clients is 4 pence per word.

Portfolios are difficult because when I've been paid the copyright passes to the client and the marketing companies I work with are reluctant to give me approval to show their competitors work I did for them. Set me a test: give me a piece to write and see what you think of it. I can also tell you that I wrote all of the text on these websites:

http://***********.com/**
http://**************.com/**
http://*****-*********.co.uk/** http://********-********-*******.com/

(That is a sample list, and not exhaustive).

Best wishes

John Lynch

Notice that there's none of that "I was very interested to see your advertisement…" stuff the Job Shop probably tells you to put in your applications. The advertiser knows you've seen the ad and assumes you are interested – why else would you be applying? I was successful with that application. Ten days later I applied for another, this time increasing the rate I wanted to 5p a word. I had no reply so I can't say whether that was because the advertiser didn't like what he saw (it was a he; at least half of the people you'll be writing for will be women and it's a mistake I suggest you don't make to suggest by the way you write that you can't see 50 percent of the world's population) or thought it was too much to pay. That's fine; at that time I wasn't prepared to take on a new client for less than that and since then my rock-bottom minimum has increased to 6p.

Chapter 5

This is a ragbag chapter; it includes all the things I want to say about freelance writing that don't fit anywhere else.

National Union of Journalists (NUJ)

Should you join? Yes, you probably should (I'm a member) – but you won't be able to until you can show them some pieces written by you in the last six months THAT HAVE YOUR NAME ON. And the drawback for freelancers who write mostly blog posts is that those blog posts almost never have your name on. (In fact, they probably almost always have someone else's name on them, because you're writing for people who want to appear as though they are the authors).

As soon as you do have the supporting evidence, it's a good idea to join. In the meantime, when you're quoting for business, use the NUJ's Freelance Fees Guide: http://tinyurl.com/ygcoxrs.

Copyright

I said in Chapter 4, "… just because you wrote something doesn't mean you have a right to reproduce it. You wrote it for a fee, you were paid, and at the moment when you were paid the copyright passed to the client. It isn't yours and you can't reproduce it in a portfolio without the client's consent. So ask." Actually, that isn't true. The copyright law in the UK says that if you wrote it, you own it. For the blog posts and web pages you will mostly be concerned with, this is not worth getting into a row about. As I've made clear, I write an awful lot of blog posts and the people I write them for almost always want them to appear as their own work. That doesn't change the law, but if you're going to do this sort of piece for money you need to accept that it is the way it is. If you want to reproduce something you wrote to show someone else, ask permission. And if you want to publish in one place something you first wrote for money to be published somewhere else, then DON'T. I can't imagine anything more unethical.

SEO and the future of blogging

I said earlier this would be something I wanted to talk about. Sometimes a client will ask me to write something and say, "This is an SEO post. Never mind the writing; it's not for human readers; just make sure the search engines like it." I think this is based on a misunderstanding of how search engines work; even if it worked, the idea of writing something without regard for how an intelligent human being might respond to it should be anathema to any writer.

If you let them, SEO specialists will reel off all sorts of metrics to show how successful a website is. In fact, in the last resort only one metric matters and that is: conversion. Whether the object of a page is to persuade someone to buy online, to build the subscription list for a newsletter, to get an invitation to visit them to discuss doing business or something else entirely, the only thing that matters is: did you get what you wanted?

On the way to that aim, ignore all the metrics of the SEO wonk and focus on just three:

- Conversation rate
- Amplification rate
- Applause rate.

Conversation Rate

No, I haven't made a mistake; I don't mean "conversion rate"; conversation rate is the number of audience comments or replies per post. It's high when you've written good stuff (which may mean good contrarian stuff – see below); you don't get comments on a badly written post unless someone is suggesting that you are Mr and Mrs Head's long lost son, Richard. You're the writer; writing that good stuff is your job. Do it well and the client will notice they get more hits on your posts which will cause them to give more work to you and not to other people.

Amplification Rate

Amplification rate is the number of retweets per tweet, the number of shares per Facebook post or the number of shares per blog post. It's what causes something to "go viral." To share your work on that scale, people have to have a reason. Giving them that reason is the writer's job.

Applause Rate

The number of likes on Facebook or a blog and the number of times a tweet is favorited. Just like the theatre, you can tell when someone liked what you did because there's more applause.

Contrarian posting

Okay, this is not in your immediate direct control because you are writing to order and the client decides what's wanted.

Look; an awful lot of blogging is a waste of time. Somebody says to you, "Put these keywords into the post you're writing for me. Don't stuff them but I need them there."

So you do that. Of course you do; if you didn't, you wouldn't get paid. The client shows those keywords to attract people who are searching for them, because people searching for those keywords are likely to be interested in what the website offers. How many other blogs do you suppose are using the same keywords to attract the same readers? A Hundred and fifty? Eight thousand? Three million? And they're all using SEO in just the same way as this website.

I have persuaded some of my clients that too many blogs say the same thing in the same way and they are both boring and unproductive. They have allowed me to write contrarian posts – that is, posts that challenge widely held but questionable reviews. And they have seen the benefit, so they've allowed me to continue.

If you find somebody who will let you do this, don't go overboard. Don't insult people. Feel free to be politically incorrect (PLEASE!) but don't commit hate crimes. That would not be ethical or productive.

Getting Paid

It's sad, but getting paid can be one of the hardest tasks for a freelancer. There are customers who don't want to pay you and others who didn't set out to stiff you but find themselves at the critical time without any money. Easier said than done, perhaps, but the best advice is: don't get into this position in the first place.

So long as you stick to their guidelines and way of working, Upwork will make sure you get paid and they have a dispute resolution process if it ever comes to that. You pay for this by giving up ten percent of your earnings and paying one dollar for every transfer, but in my view it's worth it.

If you're working on a contract, and you have any doubt about the client's ability or willingness to pay, get 50 percent up front.

Upwork or not, contract or not, make sure the scope of the work has been clearly and fully defined. Don't leave any ambiguity about what you're going to do and what you're not going to do or about what the client is committed to doing. If it comes to court, you need to make sure the client has no wriggle room arising from a lack of clarity in defining what the job was and what it wasn't. Don't leave space for the client to say, "The writer was supposed to do X, Y and Z and hasn't done it." Then it's your word against the client's and the chances are that in court you will lose.

If it comes to the crunch and you haven't been paid and the client has ignored two requests for payment (sent one week apart) get a lawyer to send a letter (I'm assuming that the debt is big enough to leave you with some income after you have paid the lawyer for the letter. If not, just forget the whole thing).

If none of that works, decide whether it's going to be worth taking court action. You'll find details on how to do that in the UK here: https://www.gov.uk/make-court-claim-for-money/overview. If your client is in another country and doesn't want to pay, you're probably going to have to forget it. Make sure you never let a debt owed to you become big enough that losing the money will damage you. Even in your own country, take a hard look at the cost of legal action and the apparent liquidity or otherwise of the client. Otherwise, you may simply be throwing good money after bad.

Time management

I have more than 30 assignments that have to be completed in the next four weeks and others are coming during that time. I owe it to the clients as well as to myself to make sure that I have a record of every assignment with its deadline and that I've arranged to be alerted as deadlines approach. One of my clients uses Basecamp, another uses Todoist and both of these send me daily alerts. I don't rely on those alone. There are many other project management software tools but time management for a freelance writer is not very complicated. We don't have Gantt charts, or tools and resources to be brought together before a job can be completed. I find Microsoft Outlook 2016 does the job just fine. Whatever method you use, you do need a way of staying abreast of every task you take on and you need to make sure that you update your schedule every day.

Drafts and revisions

When you agree a price for a job, the general consensus is that you are agreeing to provide up to two rewrites should the customer think them necessary, without extra charge.

Dealing with obnoxious clients

As with not being paid, the best advice is: don't let it happen. Don't deal with them. If only. No one avoids the occasional troublesome customer and you won't be the first. This is the point where shrinking violets either allow themselves to be driven into a mental home or learn to be more assertive.

Some rules:

1. Stick to the contract. That's why you have one and it's why you make sure that the scope of the job is clearly defined. We all have good clients for whom we stretch a point; it's when unreasonable variations are pressed on us that we realise why we wrote down in contract form what we were prepared to do for the price. When you are asked to do something that is outside the

work scoped in the contract, say, "Yes I can add that; the price that extra work will be is…"

2. You will know your own work habits; personally, I work best in the early morning and by three in the afternoon my creative well runs dry. I work for a marketing agency in California and we have very little same-day contact; they accept that and we don't have a problem. When you do have a client who expects you to be available at all hours, put boundaries around your time. This is especially important when you're in the UK and your client is in America. Or Hong Kong. Or anywhere in a different time zone. Just don't answer the phone and don't reply to text messages or emails until you're back in your own working hours.

3. Learn to say "No". Sometimes it seems the hardest word, but if you want to preserve your sanity and have time to do anything else, then when someone wants to slip just one more little job your way with a deadline that you know will be difficult to meet you need to say, "I'm sorry. This evening by eight I just can't do. Ten in the morning the day after tomorrow would be fine. Can you live with that?"

4. Never stop marketing. It's a lot easier to end relationships with difficult clients (or even with an easy one who doesn't pay enough) if you have work from elsewhere to replace them.

VAT

Should you register for VAT? Well, I'm registered and although it's an extra layer of admin and paperwork I find it improves my profit margin just enough to make it worth continuing. If all of my clients were outside the EU then there'd be less point, but I have enough UK clients now (and one in Sweden) to make it worth collecting the VAT and offsetting against it the VAT on what I buy for my freelancing business. (I reduced the net cost of my new laptop by nearly £400 that way).

If you're in America, of course, just ignore this section.

Appendix 1: Sample Freelance Writing Contract

Agreement for copywriting services

Date: **[date]**

Between me: **[Your name]** ("I", "me" or "writer" in this document)
And you: **[Client name]** ("you" or "client" in this document)

You (**[client name]**) are hiring me, **[your name]**, to **[assignment]** for a of £**[total]**.

Commitments

You confirm:

- You have the power to enter into this contract on behalf of your organisation.
- You will provide me with everything I need to complete the project, when I need it.
- You will review my work, provide feedback and sign-off within agreed timescales.
- You will abide by the payment schedule described at the end of this agreement.

I confirm:

- I will meet the terms of this agreement.
- I will keep any information you give me confidential.

Service to be delivered

I will create text and/or articles for you as described in the *assignment details* section of this agreement and deliver the text as a Microsoft Word document.

Changes and revisions

- Initial delivery of a complete copy document.
- Two subsequent rounds of changes, if required.

Copyright

Copyright passes to you when I have received full and final payment according to the terms of this agreement. Until that payment is received, copyright remains with me and no right to use the work on the Internet or in any other way passes to you. You assigned to me the right to link to the completed project on your website as part of my online portfolio.

Deadline

If this agreement is signed and I have received your down payment by **[date]**, I will deliver first draft copy by **[date]**.

Payment

The total cost of the work is: **£[amount]**

I will invoice for an initial down payment of **£[amount]** once this agreement has been signed and will start work on receipt of this payment.

I will invoice for the remaining balance of **£[amount]** once the work has been completed.

If I have not received any feedback or comments within two weeks of submitting work to you (at any stage - the initial draft or subsequent edits), I will assume you are happy the work has been completed and will invoice for the remaining balance.

I'm registered for VAT and my payment terms are 15 days.

Cancellation

If you wish to cancel this agreement, payment of the total cost of the project will become due immediately.

Although the language is simple, the intentions are serious and this contract is a legal document under exclusive jurisdiction of English courts.

Assignment

[insert full details]

Writer: **Client:**

Signed by: [name]

Signature:
....

On behalf of: [company]

Date:
....

Signature:
....

Date:
....

www.ingramcontent.com/pod-product-compliance
Lightning Source LLC
Chambersburg PA
CBHW071409080526
44587CB00017B/3228